D0862032

BEST SEAT
IN THE HOUSE

MY LIFE IN
THE JEFF HEALEY BAND

TOM STEPHEN
WITH KEITH ELLIOT GREENBERG

Published by ECW Press
665 Gerrard Street East
Toronto, Ontario, Canada, M4M 1Y2
416-694-3348 / info@ecwpress.com

Get the
eBook free!*
*proof of purchase
required

To the best of his abilities, the author has related experiences,
places, people, and organizations from his memories of them.
In order to protect the privacy of others, he has, in some
instances, changed the names of certain people and details of
events and places.

Editor for the press: Michael Holmes
Cover design: Troy Cunningham
Cover photograph by Barrie Wentzell
Author photo: © Jacqi Vené
Interior photos are from the Tom Stephen's collection
unless otherwise noted.

Purchase the print edition
and receive the eBook free!
For details, go to ecwpress.com/eBook.

Library and Archives Canada
Cataloguing in Publication

Stephen, Tom, 1955–, author
Best seat in the house : my life in the Jeff Healey Band /
Tom Stephen with Keith Elliot Greenberg.

Issued in print and electronic formats.
ISBN 978-1-77041-451-8 (softcover)
ALSO ISSUED AS: 978-1-77305-274-8 (EPUB),
978-1-77305-275-5 (PDF)

1. Stephen, Tom, 1955-. 2. Drummers (Musicians)—
Canada—Biography. 3. Healey, Jeff. 4. Guitarists—
Canada—Biography. 5. Jeff Healey Band—History. I.
Greenberg, Keith Elliot, 1959-, author II. Title.

ML419.S832A3 2018   782.42164092
C2018-902590-5   C2018-902591-3

The publication of *Best Seat in the House* has been generously supported by the Canada Council for the Arts which last
year invested $153 million to bring the arts to Canadians throughout the country, and by the Government of Canada.
*Nous remercions le Conseil des arts du Canada de son soutien. L'an dernier, le Conseil a investi 153 millions de dollars pour mettre
de l'art dans la vie des Canadiennes et des Canadiens de tout le pays. Ce livre est financé en partie par le gouvernement du Canada.*
We also acknowledge the Ontario Arts Council (OAC), an agency of the Government of Ontario, and the contribution
of the Government of Ontario through the Ontario Book Publishing Tax Credit and the Ontario Media Development
Corporation.

Ontario
Ontario Media Development
Corporation

ONTARIO ARTS COUNCIL
CONSEIL DES ARTS DE L'ONTARIO
an Ontario government agency
un organisme du gouvernement de l'Ontario

Canada Council
for the Arts

Conseil des Arts
du Canada

Canadä

PRINTED AND BOUND IN CANADA

PRINTING: NORECOB   5   4   3   2   1

MIX
Paper from
responsible sources
FSC   FSC® C103560
www.fsc.org

In Memory of Stuart Jolliffe,
1962–2018

In the end, when it's all said and done
You gotta love to live and live to love,
and you gotta have yourself some fun

"HEY HEY," JEFF HEALEY BAND

CHAPTER
one

Somewhere between Foxboro and Boston, the bus began to rock from side to side.

I was an hour or so into a rum-induced sleep, head aching as the glare from the overhead lights pushed against my eyelids. For the Jeff Healey Band, it was just another night, rolling down the highway. But something about the feel of the tour bus, shaking and shifting lanes on that icy patch of I-95, told me that, even in the twisted world of rock 'n' roll, this wasn't normal.

Falling out of my bunk, I looked down toward the front of the vehicle. We'd had problems with our drivers before. Once, in the middle of a blizzard, I caught one guy doing lines of coke on the steering wheel. I understood his thought process; after hanging out with rock stars, he believed that he could get just as screwed up, even if it meant killing the whole band — and himself. Now I saw his replacement sitting over on the wrong side of the bus.

"What the hell is he doing there?" I wondered, still partially asleep. "Are we still in England?"

Through the fog, I heard the driver's voice speaking in a soothing Texas drawl: "That's good. Just hold her steady. You're doing great. Really good, Jeff."

Jeff?

Jeff Healey was the centerpiece of our band, the best blues guitarist in the world, a man who could match — and sometimes outclass — Stevie Ray Vaughan and Eric Clapton by sitting down, opening the case of his Jackson doubleneck on his lap, and stretching his big fingers over the strings.

He also happened to be blind.

Strangely, at that moment, I wasn't too worried about Jeff's disability — my bigger concern was whether he'd been drinking or not. Either way, it was my job to put out the fire. Not only was I the Jeff Healey Band's drummer. I was the comanager. When shit happened — and a blind guy driving a 20-ton bus would definitely qualify as shit happening — the grown-ups expected me to fix the problem.

Even if, in some instances, Tom Stephen was the reason for the problem in the first place.

In this case, I quickly concluded, there was nothing I could do; I was along for the ride. When Jeff was at the wheel, both literally and figuratively, he yielded it to no one. From the moment he'd lost his vision — and his eyes — to retinoblastoma, a rare cancer that starts in the light-detecting cells of the retina, he feared nothing. Every discouraging diagnosis was taken as a challenge. At one point, I knew someone must have told him that he couldn't drive the tour bus.

It was the wrong thing to say.

Because of my unique position in the band, Jeff was in the habit of defying me like a rebellious teenager. Whatever went wrong — with the record company, the tour schedule, even the airlines — always

2

seemed to be my fault. But we looked at our band as a family and, when others came after us, no one was more loyal than Jeff.

Before we cracked the United States, we toured our native Canada from sea to sea, waking up to snowdrifts that came in through the windows and walls. But with each frigid stop, our reputation grew. During a long stretch in Vancouver, we settled in at a hotel attached to a nightclub complex that featured strippers during the day and rock 'n' roll after dark. The manager was a lovely, petite Chinese woman who treated both the talent and the customers with grace and courtesy.

We all felt protective of her, particularly Jeff.

One night, we were jamming onstage, eying a group of soldiers boozing it up pretty good. They were getting loud and becoming a nuisance. But we'd had plenty of nights like that ourselves, and weren't in a position to judge. Then one of the assholes crossed the line, grabbing the manager and tearing off the arm of her coat.

That was enough for me. I jumped over the bass drum and flew into the crowd. These guys must have seen me coming, because they grabbed me, pushed me up against a beer keg and started putting a pretty good whomping on me.

Suddenly, I heard Jeff's voice, a few feet away. "Tom?" he yelled. "Tom, where are you?"

One of the soldiers had his hands around my neck. "I'm here," I wheezed. "Right here."

Jeff took a moment to gauge where all the players were standing. Then he lifted his cane and whacked my attacker.

Boom. Boom. Out go the lights. The soldier's bros looked at him, then looked at Jeff twitching slightly, still waving his cane. The crowd went silent — pregnant pause — then broke into laughter and applause.

"Holy fuck," somebody said.

The army had been taken out by a blind guy.

Jeff was able to get away with this because he honestly didn't think of himself as handicapped. And sometimes the fans weren't sure, either. He was big and handsome and jumped around all over the stage like a maniac. He wore a pair of artificial eyes and was very particular about the color. At one gig, a girl told him that he had beautiful eyes. After that, he had friends bring him to the guy who hand-painted his eyes in Toronto to ensure the shade remained consistent. The strategy worked. The girls all thought he was cute. And our music hit hard, so the rocker guys dug him, too.

Steve Lukather, a session musician who's performed on more than fifteen hundred albums, was hanging out with the band after a show when Jeff decided to play a practical joke on him.

"Luke, come here," Jeff began, calling Steve by his nickname. "I think I have something in my eye."

When Steve bent down to check, Jeff began scratching his glass eye with his fingernail. "It traumatized me," says Lukather, who's best known for his work with the band Toto. "I tripped out. He was something else — as a man and a musician.

"I was touring with Edgar Winter — who had his sight issues himself — and I'd try to get to Jeff by banging on his hotel room door and running away. One time, he came out in his underwear and yelled, 'Fuck you, Lukather. I can *smell* you.'"

We'd be jamming with the biggest names in the world, and Jeff always managed to grab the spotlight. And I mean the *biggest* names in the world. I remember drumming behind Jeff, Eric Clapton, Keith Richards and Ron Wood. It was a kickass jam with exchanges of blistering solos. Jeff was in his zone, blowing everybody's mind. The other musicians gathered around Jeff's chair, watching him blast away. And as they came closer, I began counting because I knew what was coming.

Three, two, one . . .

Kaboom! Jeff exploded out of his chair, practically knocking the other guitarists over. It was if he'd gone bowling for rock stars and hit a perfect strike.

"His technique was original to him," remembers Slash of Guns N' Roses, "especially at that time. Playing the guitar flat on your lap

4

with two hands on the fretboard was something no one had seen at that time. He was a true phenomenon."

The first time we landed in L.A., the most beautiful women we'd ever seen were throwing themselves at Jeff. One was brilliant and came from a storied family in the music business. The bass player, Joe Rockman, and I were completely jealous. We shouldn't have been. Jeff wanted nothing to do with her.

Since Jeff was so tactile, he liked a certain type of woman — one who, to put it delicately, he could reach around and feel. The wider the better. If you were some bony model or actress, you were out. If you were nice and round, you stood a pretty good chance.

To be fair, Jeff also demanded that his women be intelligent. A pretty face meant nothing to him; he needed that extra source of stimulation. And he looked at the world through music. So he expected them to share his love of jazz and blues and rock 'n' roll.

Then again, he was as superficial as any other guy. Being voluptuous was crucial.

Shortly before a planned tour of Jamaica, I cautioned Jeff, "You know, this is going to be a little tough for you."

"What do you mean?"

"Well, you know what Jamaican men like? For the first time in your life, you're going to have to fight for these girls."

He never went.

You have to keep in mind that all three of us grew up never imagining that girls would be that interested in us. Then — almost overnight, it seemed — our live shows transformed us into lady killers. No transition. It just suddenly happened. The trick was to make sure that we didn't pursue the same girls — though many of these girls had no issue with pursuing all three of us.

To this day, I still have a hard time wrapping my head around that notion. I understand Jeff Healey. But what would some girl get out of bragging that she'd been with both Tom Stephen and Joe Rockman?

We weren't prepared for any of this. In fact, at one point, I actually had to sit Jeff down and have a serious talk with him. "Jeff," I emphasized, "you gotta wrap the rascal."

"What do you mean?"

"I mean, Jeff, you should be using protection. Are you?"

"Tom, that's none of your business. Let me look after me."

"Hey, Jeff, I'm just saying. You don't want to go home with something you didn't go on the road with."

He twisted his hair and bit his lip, like he usually did when he wasn't happy with me. That was the end of the conversation.

But a few weeks later, while we were on tour in Australia, there was a heavy pounding on my door at about 3 a.m. I opened up to see all six feet and two inches of Jeff Healey done up in Aboriginal war paint, with a girl on each side of him. It seemed like a game of Aussie trick or treat. Which it actually was.

"Simple question, Jeff," I began. "What the fuck do you want?"

Jeff was giggling like buffoon. "Tom," he announced, "I've come to wrap the monster. Do you have what I want?"

That was part of the fun of rock 'n' roll, all those unexpected moments. I also admit I enjoyed running into celebrities and having them treat me as a peer. Jeff, on the other hand, thought celebrity was bullshit. If you wanted to impress Jeff, you'd have to be a cool jazz cat. Or, at the very least, have a good story about playing music alongside a cool jazz cat. Then you were in. Jeff loved all the old-time blues players, like B.B. King, Buddy Guy and Albert Collins. He loved them and they loved him.

One night in Chicago, Jeff wanted to go to this famous blues bar on the Southside, where all the greats stopped when they were in town. But when we got in the cab, the driver warned us that we were heading to a pretty rough neighborhood.

"Do you boys really know where you're going?" he asked. And then, just in case we didn't understand subtlety, he added, "I don't know if you noticed, but you boys are white."

"I don't know too much about that," Jeff answered. "I'm blind. But I can tell you this. I like what I smell right now."

One thing I learned in the Boy Scouts: be prepared.

We happened to be at a light, just beside a chili dog restaurant. Jeff ordered the driver to pull over to the curb.

"Are you guys crazy?"

Jeff and food could never be parted. In we went. The customers seemed genuinely concerned for us. A few asked if we were lost.

"I don't know," I answered. "I'm following him."

They looked at Jeff, they looked at the cane, and they started to laugh.

No matter where you're traveling in the world, humor's a wonderful thing.

We paid for our chili dogs, returned to the cab and found our way to the club. Like the cab driver, the doorman seemed to question our logic.

"This is Jeff Healey," I pointed out, "world-famous guitarist." The doorman looked over at Jeff holding on to his cane and chomping on his hot dog.

"You boys know who *we* are?"

"That's why we're here."

"Well, it's up to you guys."

We were hanging out, grooving to the band. Jeff couldn't have been happier. He once told me that African-Americans were the "angels of the planet," explaining, "The old jazz cats, the old blues cats, they created the foundation of everything we love and care about."

Suddenly, Albert Collins himself walked in. He'd jammed with Jeff in the past, had witnessed his 15-minute version of "All Along the Watchtower," and was intrigued to see us hanging out in the hood. Of course, once the crowd noticed the type of company we kept, the mood completely changed. Jeff was lost in the music. When he liked what he heard, he had a tendency to shake his hands and direct the band. The more he drank, the more he directed, and the more fun the night became.

By this point, Joe had also caught a cab to the bar and been introduced to Albert Collins — or, as we called him, "Mr. Collins." We were all enjoying each other's companionship when Collins blurted out, "Jeff, you do realize that you're a Black man. And both of your boys with you, I think they're Black men. At least, they have some big-ass Afros."

That's the benefit, I guess, of having a Jewish bass player and a Lebanese guy behind the drums.

When Collins stepped up to the front to perform, we were invited to join him. To sit in on a session featuring Jeff Healey and Albert Collins was truly a privilege. As I was playing, the regular drummer was giving me tips. "You're not bad," he said. "But one thing you've got to figure out is the rearview mirror."

I looked at him, confused.

"You know, man. You gotta look in the rearview mirror. When you look in the rearview mirror, what you see behind you? That there's the beat."

As funny as it sounded, none of us ever forgot it. If we'd been having a bad night onstage, Jeff would shout, "Rearview mirror!" That got the point across — *pull it back, man. Pull it back.*

Jeff didn't mind putting up a battle. He fought with me enough. The fights could be good-natured or vicious. He could slice you to pieces with a phrase. I'd be scrambling for a comeback and he'd hit me with something else. Once I stooped low enough to tell him to leave the music business and sell pencils on the street corner.

He burst into laughter. He knew he was a genius and was never insecure about that stuff. Nor was he awed by the giants of our industry. And that could drive me out of my mind. When we had the chance to open for the Rolling Stones, he acted completely indifferent, mumbling something about having to do his laundry the day of the proposed gig. He didn't think they were that good — the same way he believed Hendrix was just "okay" without his stage show. I managed to convince him otherwise, and years later, he even admitted to me that the Stones were a crucial part of rock history. But before that he flat-out insulted Keith Richards's guitar playing and got us booted off a potential Rolling Stones tour.

You'll hear more about that later.

George Harrison and Mark Knopfler from Dire Straits both contributed songs to our second album. And although there was certainly a respect for all they'd accomplished, Jeff bruised some pretty big egos with his self-veneration. The same was true with Clive Davis and Ahmet Ertegun. That's Clive, the founder of Arista Records, and Ahmet, the founder of Atlantic and chairman of the Rock and Roll Hall of Fame. Both guys couldn't wait to sign Jeff Healey. And he eventually walked away from both labels. Why? Artistically, Jeff was always convinced that he was right.

Maybe he was. But, Jesus — Clive Davis and Ahmet Ertegun!

At the same time, Jeff was the greatest guy in the world, and the funniest. Late at night on the tour bus, he'd challenge everyone to that electronic game that involved shooting ducks off the screen. And he wanted to bet on it. Giving in to greed, we all took the dare.

Mick Jagger visits with the band.

Who couldn't beat a blind man at a video game? But Jeff always won, sometimes clipping us for hundreds of dollars.

"I know you're a fuckin' hustler," I told him, "I'm just trying to figure out your system."

"It's the quacks," he admitted. "I count the quacks. It's a rotation. Every time, they quack, I know where the ducks are and knock them off."

I still remember Jeff's face grinning with satisfaction. I knew he couldn't see me, but I felt that he was looking right into my eyes. When I think about moments like that, I can't believe that a man with so much life — more life than the rest of us — could leave us so quickly.

I miss him, and thank him for giving me his musical mentorship, friendship — and all the stories you're about to read here. Admittedly, some of the details may be shrouded by the haze of drugs and booze, the delirium of touring, the passage of time and the general bullshit of the music business. As best as I can tell, my recollections are true, although when I look at them objectively, they do seem pretty out there. But hey, welcome to rock 'n' roll.

Let the jam begin.

two

When you're struggling to establish yourself in a band, all you can think about is success. Once you achieve it, though, a strange phenomenon occurs. The members start to fall out of love with each other. The moment the money comes in, the parasites follow:

"You know what, Jeff? You can get a better band than that."

"You know, Tom, you really should be charging 20 percent for your management. You're the one doing all the fuckin' work."

People say that success changes you. I think about it a little bit differently. It's not so much that the people change, but the people around you change. And it magnifies your personality — both positively and negatively. No one's saying no to you. You can have most anybody you want. You can do whatever drugs you want. And if you're already kind of an asshole, you become a bigger asshole.

And that was just *us*. Imagine how this same principle applies to the Stones, Zeppelin and all those other rock 'n' roll kings. It's amazing so many are still with us.

I have a lot of respect for groups that can survive this wild ride in a "never say no" world . . . where you're used to the answer always being yes. It's so funny because when you're trying to break, the answer is no — over and over and over again. But once you get that magic yes — something most bands never experience — it all changes.

Suddenly, something that's working fine between three individuals can be obliterated. And it gets even worse when you add friends and girlfriends to the equation.

Of course, you're supposed to have wives and girlfriends and connections that go beyond rock 'n' roll. It's called maturing. But rock 'n' roll is a very immature profession. Developing other interests, the one thing that's supposed to help you grow in the straight world, diminishes the passion. In Jeff Healey's case, it was his radio show and his love of the jazz world. Joe Rockman, our bass player, was into martial arts and his workout routine. I began managing other acts. You wake up one day and realize that everyone's following his own direction, and the band isn't the priority that it should be.

But for 15 years, life in the Jeff Healey Band was great. Jeff was one of the world's most illustrious madman guitarists — who didn't give a fuck about the labels people used to describe him, but cared a lot about loyalty, honor and, above all, music. Even through the stresses and the hard times, we had a default setting that allowed us to ignore the stupid fights, take care of business and perform like nobody else.

This is a story about three nerds who came together and made a band. Like most rock 'n' roll tales, it doesn't have a happy ending. But our music kicked ass. We were gods among men. And with a blind lead singer, we definitely beat the odds.

Because of my role in the Jeff Healey Band, I was the lightning rod for everything that went wrong. As a result, some people say I'm not qualified to tell our story at all. But they can't diminish all the time that Jeff and I spent together from the time we founded the band — touring, performing, partying, laughing, fighting and talking. It didn't end pretty, but we knew each other intimately. And that entitles me, perhaps more than anybody, to tell the Jeff Healey Band story, warts and all. Frankly, I no longer care what anyone thinks. The three of us made great things happen, and I will not allow others to reinvent history. They weren't there, nor did they pay their dues for that right.

When I think back to the period that I romanticize the most, my mind drifts to early 1986. We had money in the bank — a rarity for a band — our own independent label to promote our songs, and a growing reputation in clubs all around Canada. We were still waiting for one of the big labels to sign us. But it was coming.

We could all feel it.

In Calgary one night, we talked our way backstage at a Stevie Wonder concert. I was shameless in maneuvering this, emphasizing that Jeff also was blind and heavily suggesting that Stevie was his hero. When the two finally met, though, Jeff was disappointed. Here he was, walking around backstage, introducing himself to strangers, and Stevie had a handler on each side, guiding him to the hands he was supposed to shake. As we left the building, Jeff turned to me and said, "What a wuss. He can't get around a room without people to push him and pull him."

Of course, years later, Jeff was blown away when Stevie Wonder asked him to jam. The reality was that Stevie was a star, and he would have had people doing almost as much if he'd been sighted. But the experience reminded Jeff of some of the cautious kids he remembered from the School for the Blind in Brantford, Ontario. He interpreted the overindulgence as helplessness and weakness.

When Jeff had that fire in his belly, he could rival Jimi Hendrix or Stevie Ray Vaughan. He was that good. There was also no better self-promoter, and I say this not with cynicism but with reverence. Jeff had been onstage since he was a child and was accustomed to being on the radio and TV. He was a musicologist who could talk endlessly about the history of his craft. These were skills that I hadn't even calculated when I made the decision to leave my prior career and devote myself to music.

In every town, Jeff would walk into the radio station with his guitar and serenade the DJ. If the guy wasn't a believer beforehand, by the time we were going down the stairs you'd hear our record being played.

Our hustle was the same as the hip hop guys today, going corner to corner and bugging people, selling our single from the car, stage, street corner, whatever it took. If you have the right product, they eventually listen.

Steve Herman, the senior vice president of Live Nation USA, was a young agent we met when we rented a booth at a college entertainment convention. "The college market was still a significant market for development," he says. "Most colleges had big bars and theaters in them, so a group like the Jeff Healey Band could do 30 to 40 shows a year on college campuses. This was just supposed to be an event for agents, buyers and business types. But these guys rented the space as a 'company,' set Jeff up and let him wail.

"When he touched that guitar, it was like David Gilmour — you could *feel* him when he played. You were like, 'Wow, where did this kid come from?' He was just meant to be up there. When he was on the stage, you could see how happy he was.

"First the organizers came and shut off the music. Then everybody lined up to sign them up for gigs."

Back home in Toronto, we picked up a gig at the Diamond Club. It was bigger and more prestigious than a lot of places that we'd played. By this point, the word was out in the industry that we were on the verge, and when Dr. John came to town, we were told that he wanted us as his backup band.

This was a huge deal for our fans. Later on, Jeff wasn't fazed when we met the president of the United States or the Queen of England. But this was one of the few times that I ever saw him nervous before a gig. He rated Dr. John as one of the greats, a classic songwriter and piano player who not only represented the New Orleans tradition but *knew* Louis Armstrong. Jeff was humbled to be linked to that history.

Dr. John was equally enthusiastic about sharing the stage with Jeff. All night long, he'd turn to the audience and ask, "How do you like my band?" Of course, the fans would scream their approval — louder every time Dr. John asked. Dr. John was enamored with Jeff's innovation and musicianship, and told him so backstage. It was love.

About once a week, we'd play this smaller club called Clinton's. One night, I felt a buzz go through the building before we went out onstage. When I asked what was going on, someone breathlessly told me that Bob Dylan was at a table downstairs. It wasn't hard to figure out how he knew about us. Dylan was plugged into the music scene in Toronto because of his relationship with the Band, whose front man, Robbie Robertson, grew up playing some of the same venues as us.

After the show, a very attractive female came backstage and informed us that Bob Dylan wished to meet Jeff. At first, Jeff didn't know whether to believe it. So I went into the crowd, and yes, Dylan was there, donned in a stocking hat and these round glasses a middle-aged woman might wear on a vacation to Disney World.

I introduced myself and invited him backstage. "No," Dylan growled. "He has to come down."

When I conveyed the message, Jeff got angry. "Fuck Bob Dylan," he said.

It was a stalemate. I was thinking about how great it would be if photos of the two circulated — the icon and the icon-in-the-making. But Jeff couldn't be budged.

Eventually, we were told, Dylan left.

Jeff was unmoved. "Eh," he shrugged. "Whatever."

As much as I respected Jeff for standing his ground and being contemptuous of the cult of celebrity, I was really mad. "Jeff," I argued. "This is Bob fuckin' Dylan. This could have been the thing that got us our record deal."

"He's not that fuckin' great."

"But we play 'All Along the Watchtower.' Play it to death. And

'Like a Rolling Stone.' You love that song. He's the writer. Why couldn't you have gone over to him, as a tribute?"

"He came here to see me, and I played. *That's* his tribute."

Never mind that, when Jeff's defenses were down a few years later, he called Dylan one of rock 'n' roll's greatest composers.

We had a far better experience with B.B. King — even though a misdeed by one of my family members almost derailed the whole thing.

With the money we'd been saving, we decided to fly out to Expo 86, a World's Fair in Vancouver. We were promised a two-week gig, and we arrived in western Canada expecting to mingle and jam with a lot of big names. But when we stopped at the venue to check it out, I noticed that the place was under renovation.

I stepped over construction equipment and went looking for the manager. "What's going on with the club?"

"Oh, we decided we're not doing blues anymore. We're becoming a country place."

"When?"

"We're planning to reopen again in three weeks. Who are you guys?"

I felt both dread and fury. "We're the band that's supposed to be playing here."

"You mean, nobody told you?"

This actually wasn't management's fault. In order to appear in Vancouver at Expo 86, I'd contacted a local agent, who spoke effusively about the great exposure we'd receive. We'd taken a risk and spent our money on airfare. The club was going to cover our lodging and the rest of our expenses. At least, that's what we'd been told.

"Shit. Where are we going to stay?"

It didn't make business sense for a club, in the midst of an expensive construction project, to put up a band it no longer wanted. But out of benevolence, the manager did offer to assist us. If we wished, he said, we could sleep in a boardroom — on three separate cots.

I took a breath to compose myself, and looked over at Joe and Jeff. Although Jeff couldn't see, I could tell that he was glaring at me.

The first thing I did was track down the agent. Not surprisingly, he refused to come to the phone. So I staked out his office and waited until I saw him in the street. Then I began threatening him.

"Either you fix this, or I'm going straight to my biker buddies." I didn't know any bikers in Vancouver. "When they find out what happened, how you screwed us, you will be dead. I'm not saying this as a figure of speech. You will be dead."

"No, no, no," he replied. "I'll get you something at Expo." He began thinking quickly. "There's a band I was working with, an American band. They were supposed to be doing a lunchtime slot at Expo, but they had a car accident." He seemed happy about this. "I don't think they're going to make it."

Incredibly, he was telling the truth. He did find us a spot on the grounds of Expo 86. But at lunchtime our audience consisted of blue-hairs and toddlers in strollers — or "silver heads" and "ankle biters," as Jeff called them. When Jeff started rocking out, the audience complained.

"Turn the music down," they'd yell over their eight-dollar French fries. "It's too loud."

Despite this, Jeff was happy now that we were jamming. With every gripe, he'd smile and turn the volume louder.

For me, it was a total drag. But not only were we getting paid, we had our own hotel rooms. And while we were in town, a musician friend suggested that we check out B.B. King's show on the Expo main stage.

After what we'd just endured, I wasn't going to settle for being a member of the audience. When I asked the agent for backstage passes, he told us that the request was "impossible." As a result, I decided to use some more of our savings and hire a limousine to take us to the back gate. When we got there, I rolled down the window a crack and flashed the pass that indicated we were authorized to perform for the lunch crowd.

"Those passes aren't good here," one of the guards said.

I acted incredulous. "We're performers at Expo," I explained. "Did someone screw up and give us the wrong passes again?" I began muttering to myself. "This happens in every city."

The guard appeared sympathetic. "Well, the passes do say you're 'day talent' . . ."

"I know it's not your fault, man. But, shit, B.B.'s not going to be happy to hear that his blind buddy can't get backstage."

The guard checked out the limo. "Stevie Wonder?"

I said nothing as the guard contemplated a few seconds, then opened the gate and waved us in, following our vehicle on foot. When this tall, blond man got out with his guitar case, instead of Stevie Wonder, the guard began to protest.

"Hey, that's not . . ."

I pushed Jeff into the building.

Backstage, we walked up and down the hallways, trying to find B.B. Now it was Jeff's turn to take over. When we discovered the location of B.B.'s dressing room, Jeff planted himself outside, opened his guitar case in his lap and started banging away on the strings.

Within minutes, B.B.'s road manager was standing in front of Jeff, listening. "Wow," he said. "What are you guys doing here?"

Jeff continued playing.

"I don't know," I answered. "I thought that Mr. King might want to meet Jeff."

"Jeff?" The man's face crinkled up. "Jeff *who*?"

I motioned at Jeff, playing his guitar. "Jeff Healey," I stated. "You mean, you haven't heard of Jeff Healey?"

The man seemed completely confused. "Maybe," he responded. "I'll check with B.B."

As the manager disappeared into the dressing room, Jeff smiled in my direction, launching into another song. Fifteen minutes passed. Then a half hour. The manager left the room at one point — without looking at us — then went back inside. Finally, the door opened and a hand motioned us forward.

There B.B. sat. "Jeff Healey," he said. "Play me something, Jeff."
Jeff laid this wicked fucking lick down the neck of his guitar.

B.B. tipped his head back. "My, my." Then he grinned. "Son, I've never seen anything like this. What are you guys doing?"

"Oh," I answered, acting like we were big shots. "We're here at Expo. Playing the lunchtime slot."

B.B. studied me for a long time. Then I noticed a spark in his eye. "Haven't I met you before?"

I was stunned. When I was a teenager, my cousin tried to promote a series of shows with B.B. in the Queen Elizabeth High School auditorium in Halifax. It was a disaster. It began with B.B. missing his flight from Boston — and the first gig. Then, after he arrived for the next concert, the limo broke down, and I ended up driving B.B. around in my 1977 Trans Am.

"Well, Mr. King," I started to answer, "I once drove you around Halifax . . ."

"I remember. Bucky. Bucky Adams was there. He was the sax player." He paused. "Do you know that your cousin is the only man who's ever sued me in my career?"

I felt worse than I had in the debris-laden nightclub. Considering everywhere he'd traveled, how could B.B. King possibly remember what I looked like from sitting in my Trans Am for a few hours — years ago, when I was just out of high school? We'd gone all this way, and to all this expense, to get turned away because of a sin one of my crazy Lebanese relatives committed on the other side of Canada. What were the chances?

B.B. turned his attention back to Jeff. "Tell you what," he began. "Why don't you come back tomorrow night?" Jeff nodded and started to close his guitar case. Was this a diplomatic way of blowing us off? Then Mr. King had another thought.

"In fact, why don't you come up and jam with me tonight?"

By morning, everyone in Vancouver had heard of Jeff Healey. When B.B. brought him onstage the next night, Jeff had been

Jeff and B.B.

officially anointed. For the duration of the band, B.B. would remain a consistent supporter.

"You've got a guy there named Jeff Healey and there's none better than him," he'd tell the *Toronto Star*. "He's my friend, too . . . Pass the word on him. I love that guy."

I can't emphasize enough what this meant to Jeff. "This was as close as I imagine being onstage with someone like (Louis) Armstrong would have been like," he told *Guitar Player*.

The crappy agent took credit for everything. But we weren't mad at him anymore. Instead of coming home at the end of Expo 86, we stayed in Vancouver for a month. But there were no more geriatrics and preschoolers in the crowd. We played all the top rooms, left with heavy pockets and flew home to Toronto in business class.

We still didn't have our record deal. But that's where we were going. B.B. King saw it. Dr. John saw it. Even fuckin' Bob Dylan saw it.

Soon, the rest of the world would, too.

three

Jeff's father, Bud, always said that his son did things his own way. Bud was a salt-of-the-earth guy, a decent, honest, principled man who worked as a firefighter and raised his family in the Etobicoke district in western Toronto. He and his wife, Yvonne, a nurse, adopted Jeff not long after his birth in 1966 — he also had two adopted sisters — even though they knew that he had cancer in one eye. The cancer quickly spread to the other eye and, with medical technology being what it was at the time, the Healeys were advised to take a drastic step: removing both eyes before Jeff was even two years old. Sadly, it would be cancer that would eventually end Jeff's young life.

This tells you a lot about the fiber of the Healeys. They'd opted to raise a child who was not only sightless but eyeless. You could say that they didn't have much of a choice. What were they supposed to do, label their child defective and bring him back? But the Healeys really understood their son, even when he was tiny, insisting that he live as independently as possible.

Jeff liked to tell the story about Bud trying to help his son navigate his surroundings. But Jeff would scold his father, "Don't guide me." When Jeff's buddies leapt from 15-foot walls, he joked, he'd protect himself and jump from nothing higher than 10 feet.

Jeff wasn't kidding. He was fearless.

I always had the impression that Bud and Yvonne considered themselves blessed to have such a strong-willed, talented child. And I'm convinced that Jeff thrived largely because he was fortunate to grow up in the Healey household.

Bud and Yvonne were country-and-western-type people, and very early on, they noticed something interesting about Jeff. He'd respond to the music he heard at home by moving his feet, his arms and his torso to the sounds coming out of the record player. Jeff said that his parents contemplated purchasing a piano for their son but didn't have the money. So when he was three, he received his first guitar, a small acoustic one, for Christmas. With great patience, Bud taught Jeff how to use a slide to tune and alter the guitar chords.

Still, it was Jeff who taught himself how to play. "I never looked at the guitar as being a serious thing," he told the British magazine *Guitarist* in 1989. "It was just something in addition to all the other things I had around the house . . . harmonicas, little horns, toy pianos and stuff like that. So while music in general has always been a part of my life, I've never looked at myself as being singularly a guitarist. More of just a musician."

Because of his size, he couldn't get his arm around the guitar. So he'd place it on his lap and spread his hands over the strings, using all five fingers for different types of vibrato. Not coincidentally, it's similar to the way people read braille, pushing into the indentations. But Jeff was also developing a unique style of playing.

"I've never tried to put what I do into words," he explained. "From a purely physical viewpoint, you can say that I play with both hands over the top of the guitar, with the left hand doing the fretting and the right hand doing the picking."

When someone plays guitar in a regular format, the thumb is not part of the action. By contrast, as Jeff aged and became a big man with huge hands, he incorporated both thumbs, playing octaves, inventing his own chords, his own notes. "If I want to make a large bend, I might brace my thumb against the neck and do it with the index or middle finger," he explained.

This wasn't slide guitar. The instrument was tuned like a regular guitar. But Jeff attacked it in his own way. And because he was playing from the top of the frets, he never fought gravity. Gravity worked with him.

Going down is easier than going up — something I'd learn all too well later on.

A lot of people were quick to deride Jeff's unique guitar-playing style as gimmickry. But Jeff was emphatic about the fact that, at the beginning at least, he held his instrument on his lap for comfort. As he put it, "That's all I know."

Either way, no one's ever played the guitar that way before or since.

"It doesn't matter how someone is holding an instrument, as long as they're getting good tones," he explained in one interview.

As with B.B. King, Jeff's living guitar heroes would all stare in wonder while listening to those tones. It was Stevie Ray Vaughan who said, "This guy is going to revolutionize the way the guitar is played."

At times, Jeff would be asked if he felt that being blind gave him a distinct advantage over other artists. The question annoyed him, but he generally answered patiently that the advantage came from his imagination. Without this, he'd continue, pointing at his head, there'd be little that he couldn't do with his fingers. I later heard many of the girls on the road agree.

By the time Jeff was five or six, he was something of a child prodigy, playing in legion halls in a cowboy hat, mimicking the styles of

Chet Atkins and Luther Perkins, the right hand picking and strumming, the left running across the strings of the headboard.

"My parents were never the sort to overdo it by throwing all sorts of praise around," he recalled, "because that kind of thing never does you any real good. It just makes you start believing you're a lot better than you really are. They were just happy that I found something at an early age that was amusing for me."

By age nine, he began expanding his interests to blues and jazz. He had a mentor, Stephen C. Barr, a guy in his thirties, a bit of a drunk who worked odd jobs, but brilliant. He loved jumping onstage and playing blues harmonica, and he was definitely a jazz snob. Barr starting turning Jeff on to performers from the 1920s. During his lonely moments at home, the jazz kept Jeff company, and I think he pictured himself back in time, playing trumpet in one of the big bands, hanging out with his idols, like Bix Beiderbecke, Fletcher Henderson, Artie Shaw, Ethel Waters, Lionel Hampton and his favorite, Louis Armstrong. The old-time jazz definitely contributed to Jeff's character. He became a record collector; he'd identify specific discs by the grooves going into the label and the grooves underneath the paper.

Jeff was extremely organized. On the road, my room would be a mess — I'd wake up with strangers lying on the floor next to trays of old food, and smoke so thick that I could barely find the door — but Jeff had everything neatly ordered. Similarly, his albums were arranged alphabetically, with the compilations at the very end. "It might take me a little while to think of where I put, say, a studio band recording that I play very little," he said. "But all the good stuff — all the jazz and things like that — I know exactly where that is."

Some of his records came from his grandmother, who inherited them from her father-in-law. When relatives became aware of this interest, they began scavenging through their attics and adding to Jeff's archive. He was so young at the time, he hadn't realized that there was a whole network of people who lived for this stuff, searching for gems in secondhand record stores and flea markets.

"When I was a kid, my dad told me if I'd put one quarter the effort into my school work as I did into my records, I would have been an A student, which I probably would have," he told journalist Coral Andrews. "But I didn't see any reason for it. What's the point of being an A student? It's the same as making a lot of money. It doesn't really achieve anything for you, except you get a lot of money."

Jeff was never motivated by money. And as honorable as it is, that caused us some problems later on.

Unlike other kids, who want to break away from their families, Jeff loved visiting his grandmother and listening to her vaudevillian comedy records from the teens and '20s. To Jeff, anything that came out after the 1940s was uncool.

He was getting a lot of attention by this stage. There wasn't a song that Jeff couldn't play on guitar — he received an inexpensive knockoff of a Gibson SG at age 11 — including R&B. All he had to do was hear a song once on the radio, and he knew the guitar part, the chords, the lead. But when people saw him play, they were confused about the way he held the guitar.

A few of them got into Bud's ear: "Oh my God. The kid's talented, but he's learning guitar the wrong way. You better get him lessons." Canadian jazz great Oscar Peterson felt that, if Jeff didn't change his style, he'd never progress any further.

Bud sought out other opinions. Within the small community where Jeff was known, Bud rounded up some of the local guitar legends.

"Leave him alone," Jeff's father was told. "He's a phenomenon."

Jeff's parents thought that they were making the right decision by sending him to the School of the Blind. But he didn't like it. It was a boarding school, and Jeff missed day-to-day interactions with his warm, supportive family. However, it was at the Brantford, Ontario, school that someone showed Jeff standard guitar tuning. He also learned braille and other essential skills that a blind person needs in order to function.

I'm not sure if they trained the students to work with guide dogs, but I'm positive Jeff would have rejected the overture. Jeff had issues with animals and never liked dogs that much. If someone did try to pair him with a retriever, I'm sure Jeff told them he preferred the company of humans.

Nonetheless, Jeff made friendships at the School for the Blind that lasted for decades; some of his buddies were still around when we formed our band. As a rule, though, he felt that the blind kids were unnecessarily pampered. Jeff didn't just aspire to be a regular guy. He already was one, and resented the way blind people were pitied and favored. So it wasn't difficult for him to convince his parents to send him to a public high school.

But his time in Brantford left an impression. When people told Jeff that, surely, he was so talented because his blindness heightened his other senses, he referred to the kids in music class at the School for the Blind. "Half of these guys couldn't carry a fucking note," he once told me, "let alone play an instrument."

But being the only blind kid in Etobicoke Collegiate high school was also a challenge. Some guys made him the butt of their jokes and tripped him when he walked by. Jeff never forgot it, and carried around an anger that I personally understood. I knew the same kinds of jackasses, and both of us were going to show those jerks the type of prowess we had — proving our self-worth by selling out concert halls and meeting more girls than these guys could ever imagine.

You couldn't really marginalize Jeff for long. He did some theater at the school, and even scored a few TV roles — something you'd think he would have bothered mentioning a few years later, when we made *Road House*. Because he was a natural leader, Jeff began to stand out from his peers as a phenomenon in his high school band. Without question, Jeff was the greatest guitarist that the students — and the teachers — had ever seen. And soon the hottest girls in the school were ignoring the bullies and flocking to Jeff.

"I guess guitar was the salvation I had from being classified as just plain weird," he told *Music Scene* magazine. "Being the only blind person at your school can get you a strange reputation. Most people thought I descended from outer space."

But Jeff's reputation — both on and off the school grounds — only enhanced his popularity. The kid was becoming a celebrity. He was about 14 the first time he played in a nightclub, filling in for a missing guitarist and singing backup. The CBC's *Fresh Air* radio show created a feature centered around Jeff, a blind high schooler with a sophisticated taste in old records. Jeff talked about his favorite songs and played a few for the audience.

He liked the attention, of course. But, as a true musicologist, he savored those moments when he could be alone with his records. He listened to Jimi Hendrix, Jeff Beck and Buddy Guy, played trumpet — even at the height of the Jeff Healey Band, he'd occasionally grab his trumpet and sit in with Dixieland bands in the various cities we visited — and began fantasizing about the types of guitars he'd eventually play onstage: the Jackson 6- and 12-string doubleneck, as well as the black Fender Squier Strat and white standard Strat.

Many of Jeff's new friends were jazz snobs like his mentor, Stephen C. Barr — very opinionated guys who insisted that rock 'n' roll was a waste of time. At times, Jeff embraced this attitude himself. In fact, it was one of the factors that later broke up the Jeff Healey Band.

The truth was that Jeff could not be contained to one genre. "I played a little bit of R&B," he said in *Musician* magazine. "I did a heavy metal jam session once . . . You get a little transistor amp, distort the hell out of it, play what you know, and you've got heavy metal.

"One night, I even did a pickup gig with a reggae band . . . When I went to the gig, the guy said, 'Now, when you're playing, just imagine that, between every beat, somebody's passing you a joint. You've got to take the joint, take a drag and give it back in that time frame, so it's tight and relaxed.'"

He was still in high school when he joined a blues group called Blue Direction, and became part of the scene in downtown Toronto. He'd later describe the blues to journalist Lisa Zimmer as "a feeling . . . one of the best forms of open improvisation . . . I mean, you've got 12 bars and a pretty standard change around those, and you could sort of do what you want with it."

Jeff was tall and his voice was no longer high, but most of the crowd probably realized that he was underage. However, when those fingers touched the strings, no one cared.

Grossman's Tavern was kind of a dump, where they never checked IDs and you could smoke joints in the audience, but it was a genuine Toronto landmark, founded by the Grossman family in 1948 on Spadina Avenue when it was the center of the city's Garment District and Jewish community. Eventually, the Louie family took over Grossman's and became Jeff's fiercest supporters. The whole atmosphere was bohemian, loose and cool. This guy named Corey Milhailiuk, a photographer who was part of the local music circuit, was the first one to bring Jeff to Grossman's. And it was there that the seeds of his greatness were sown.

By the time I met Jeff, he'd dropped out of high school, but was privately studying music theory, harmony and arranging. And his fame was growing. He was 19 when he and a friend went to see Texas blues master Albert Collins at a Toronto club called Albert's Hall. Because Jeff was regarded as a local phenom, Collins decided to humor him and let the kid sit in for one song. Jeff stayed up there an hour. He did so well that, three nights later, Collins asked Jeff to perform with him again, this time alongside Stevie Ray Vaughan.

I guess I was attracted to people who were fighting the law of averages. When I first met Jeff, I was playing in a band with one of the best guitar players in Toronto, Buzz Upshaw, one of those musicians who, under different circumstances, might have been world famous. His style was reminiscent of Albert King, Buddy Guy, Otis Rush and others, and he was a staple in Toronto for a quarter century. Buzz had the talent, but not the looks. He was a heavy-set guy who worked full time driving a garbage truck. And one of his feet was shorter than the other.

Both Jeff and Buzz clearly wanted to compensate for their respective disabilities. But there's a beauty in music that allows you to use

Albert Collins and Stevie Ray Vaughan going out of their minds watching Jeff.

it as a place to express inner feelings. I know that's the way it was for Jeff and Buzz, as well as for me.

Jeff was a fan of Buzz, and would come to our gigs at a local hamburger joint. Eventually, I was invited to jam with Jeff at Grossman's. Jeff was just a kid, maybe 17 going on 18. But he tore the place up. Onstage, he'd run all over the place, knocking things over. When the show was over, I said, "Man, how come you play so good when you're so fucked up?"

Jeff seemed to stare right through me. He curled his lips into a smirk, like a drunk preoccupied with thoughts far away from your conversation. Then he replied, "What do you mean 'fucked up?' I'm blind." Oops!

Again, remember that Jeff didn't walk around in shades. And he didn't shake his head from side to side like Stevie Wonder. As I got to know him better, I'd notice that when he was tense, he'd bite his lip or curl the back of his hair.

Over the next few months, Buzz and I would play with Jeff often. I had a straight job at the time, and a master's degree in urban planning, and it was killing me to get home from a gig at 7 a.m., shower and go to work. But when I thought about doing music full time, I knew that Buzz wasn't my ticket. He liked his job in sanitation and was looking forward to his pension. Despite his immeasurable skills, gigging was a hobby. Never once did he venture into the studio to record his music. The best I could do was to convince him to allow someone else to record our live shows so we could distribute the tapes to get gigs at other clubs. So when Jeff asked me to become his full-time drummer, I took it seriously — with a couple of reservations.

"Look, if we do this, we have to have a management strategy," I said. "I don't want to be playing in Grossman's Tavern the rest of my life. You're the most amazing musician I've ever seen. You need to get a record deal."

"I can't get a record deal. Everybody in Canada's turned me down."

"Well, if I go full time with you, I'm going to do everything to change that."

I didn't know how, but I knew that I was going to do it. Aware that I'd need to make some sacrifices, I decided to move into a cheaper apartment. Rather than feeling slighted by my decision, Buzz graciously offered to help me move. I enlisted some other friends, but when they didn't show up on time, Jeff volunteered, too.

All of my stuff was in garbage bags, and as we were walking down the steps, I'd hear crashing and smashing and cursing. But I couldn't exactly tell my helpers to take it easy. After all, I'm the one who chose a blind guy and a 400-pound handicapped dude as moving men. On top of that, we got stoned and lost the van.

But I was raised to take any way but the easy route.

CHAPTER
four

I grew up hearing myself referred to as a "wog" and "sand nigger," references to my Lebanese heritage that could only be countered with a fist to the face. The reality is that my ancestry is slightly more complicated. My mother's part-Scottish. But I guess it's a little bit like being part-Black. When people know that you have that Lebanese blood, you're reminded of it constantly.

I got a lot of my drive from my paternal grandfather and namesake, Thomas. In Canada, he saw streets of manure and mud, and decided to pave them with gold — well, gold for *him*, anyway — opening one of the first asphalt plants in eastern Canada with his brothers. Eventually, the family owned five factories but, of course, by then the kids were involved and it was a goddamn mess, with everybody suing each other. Still, he gave a lot of jobs to French-Canadians and Blacks and other people no one else would hire, and allowed them to build a beachhead for their families. A lot of Lebanese families got their start with him.

My father, Wally, definitely had his issues, but I understand why my mom, Rose — everyone called her "Wild Rose," and it was from her that I inherited my musical and artistic abilities — was attracted to him. He was an athlete who played rugby and was scouted by the Boston Red Sox. Like me, he was a drummer, playing the snare in parades sponsored by Lebanese-Christian organizations formed to promote ethnic pride and, when necessary, sway politicians. After college, he went to law school. By the time he graduated, though, he was already in the asphalt business.

He told me that he had taken on exactly one case, and lost.

In reality, he would have been happier a generation earlier, opening up a couple of grocery stores and buying some properties the old

My grandparents Thomas and Fema Stephen.

My father's law school graduation.

33

Daddy's home-time to play

*That's my mom's handwriting at
the bottom on the photo.*

Lebanese way. Instead, he was influenced by his loyalty to the family to keep Stephen Construction going. The pressure was enormous. His marriage to my mom ended — she'd marry another four times — and, if truth be known, he was an alcoholic. But both parents gave me more love and support than I could have asked for under the circumstances, educating and instilling in me a strong sense of right and wrong.

So I grew up in a family whose dysfunction would mirror the relationships you usually form in a rock 'n' roll band. There was substance abuse, fractured marriages, anger and a lot of sadness. But there were also laughs and excitement — the things that keep bands going. My dad would seat the dog on his knee and they'd go for drives, stopping at this steakhouse named Randy's. The dog was allowed to eat in the restaurant while my father got loaded. Once, when they were coming home, they barreled into the driveway without slowing down, hit all the garbage cans and crashed through the wooden garage door. I ran outside to see a shattered, smoking mess.

"Jesus Christ," I heard my dad mutter to the dog. "I thought you could drive this thing."

Needless to say, years later, when Jeff decided to take the wheel of the tour bus, there was a touch of déjà vu.

As a small child, I developed a rare kidney disease, and was expected to die. Then, around Christmastime, I rallied. It was a Christmas miracle. I know so because that's what the local newspaper called it. My photo was on the front page. I was in the hospital bed, and next to me, on the tray, was a toy monkey playing the drums.

Little did I know that I'd be that monkey one day.

My first set of Cadet drums came from a pawnshop. They were red and black, and a present for Christmas. It may have been the best Christmas of my life — although I'm not sure anyone else in the family was having much fun, listening to me hit the drums nonstop for the entire winter break. I think my parents were really happy to see me go back to school.

Drummers are a rare breed. As the saying goes, we're like mushrooms — kept in the dark and covered in shit. When we meet each other, there's an instant bond. Every day, we're the ones onstage being yelled at: "Slow down. Speed up. Do it this way. Try it another way." In essence, we're expected to play every way except the way we actually feel it. And we're not supposed to sulk and bring down the mood of the band. So we develop a thick skin and a sense of humor… at least, sometimes.

We've been around since the time of the cavemen. I know people call prostitution the world's oldest profession. But I disagree. Drummers came first. Those girls had to dance to somebody.

Yet, as a kid, I never imagined that I'd make a living onstage; Jeff's was my first "professional" band at the ripe age of 28. I was destined, it seemed, to work in the family business. From the time I was 13, in 1968, I stopped whatever else I was doing and shoveled asphalt all summer. But something was always pulling me toward music. My hometown, Saint John, New Brunswick, was close to Maine, where a lot of African-American airmen were stationed. Maine was a pretty white-bread place, and these guys didn't want to

With my little brother and sister.

get into fights every night for dancing with white girls. So they'd come up to our part of Canada, where there was an entrenched Black population, and bring the blues and R&B with them. One of my fondest childhood memories is sitting in the Lily Lake Pavilion with my dad, listening to the blues. Because of this influence, a lot of the white musicians I knew gravitated to what was traditionally Black music.

I credit my sister, Vivian, with getting me further into the *blooze* a few years later when she bought me a Dutchy Mason record. Dutchy was practically unknown in other parts of the world, but in Canada he's known as the prime minister of blues. He was a magical guy who, naturally, drank too much, complicated his personal life and was never shy about taking advantage of those around him. Once, my cousin — the concert promoter who sued B.B. — booked Dutchy in Montreal. The plan was for his drummer, Ainslie "A.J." Jardine, to pick him up on the way in from Halifax. But A.J. and Dutch were both wildmen whose minds operated in a different stratosphere. When A.J. was loading his drums into the club, my cousin asked about Dutchy.

"Damn," A.J. answered. "I knew I forgot something." Or so the story goes.

The guy had driven all the way from Halifax to Montreal without the leader of the band. Welcome to the *blooze*.

All the great music today — from rock to hip hop — comes from the blues. As the saying goes, the blues had a baby and called it rock 'n' roll. And music was just one part of it. It was also defiance. And it was sex.

My babysitter, Connie, had a boyfriend, Burton, who drove a Harley and loved rock 'n' roll. His favorite band was the Dave Clark Five, especially the song "Bits and Pieces," which had a long, drawn out snare shot: *da, da, da, da, da, da, da, da, da, da, da.* When Connie and Burton thought I was sleeping, they'd listen to the Dave Clark Five and fool around. Once, I caught them in the act. That was the beginning of my fascination with motorcycles, garter belts and drum solos.

In eighth or ninth grade, a group of guys near me learned a few chords and songs and labeled themselves a band. Even though they already had a drummer, they invited me to join. This was a big social opportunity for me; these guys were considered cool, and I was hoping that some of that would rub off on me. They sold me on the idea that the band would have two drummers. The reality was that the original percussionist needed my gear so he could have a double-bass drum kit. Essentially, I became a drum roadie, lugging my stuff from place to place.

I was oblivious to this until a girl named Diane asked, "Hey, Tommy, why don't you ever play anything?" When I raised this question with the bandleader, he responded, "Sorry, Tom, these songs are highly rehearsed."

Keep in mind that these guys only knew three chords. So I issued an ultimatum. I'd practice and learn a few songs. But if I wasn't included in the show, the main drummer would be back down to a single-bass drum kit.

Following my logic, the bandleader granted me the privilege of playing two songs a night.

My first gig took place in a little peninsula town — in front of two girls, a few farmers and a lot of cows, with the power regularly shorting out. As you'll read later, I'd later have a similar experience in the Jeff Healey Band, when we played a festival where the people seemed to be outnumbered by cattle. On this particular day — after we got stoned out of our trees — the sight of all those animals gave me the inspiration to name our group Battery Operated Electric Cow.

I wouldn't say that we gained any kind of fame. But we scored a few more gigs, prompting my mother to buy me one of those sparkly shirts to wear onstage. Girls would actually come to my house — two or three at a time — knock on my door, and ask to see the sparkly shirt. The lesson: girls and music went together.

To me, sensuality and rock music were always intertwined. Same with hip hop. There's a sexual energy that the performer gives the audience and takes with him off the stage. And it's reciprocated at the end of the night when he runs into the ladies who've seen the show. At the same time, the dudes want to party and hang. I had guys offer me their wives in Scotland, their Harleys in Texas and everything in between. There were no rules in this full-time decadent Disneyland, where everything went — fast!

• •

A friend of mine once told me, "Tom, it's not so much that you're a bullshit artist or, for that matter, even a great storyteller. You're just one of those guys the story falls all around, good or bad."

When I was 15, I watched my friend, Noel Winters, grab my pellet gun and try to shoot a guy off a motorcycle. And this was a guy he liked! Already a well-known hood, Noel was so charming that he became one of my father's drinking buddies. Around the same time, he confided to me about a deal he had going on with the captain of this boat in the harbor. He was going to make a lot of money, he said, and needed my help.

"What do you want me to do?"

"Translate."

"Translate what?"

"These guys are Egyptian."

"Yeah, so what? I'm Canadian."

"But you're Lebanese."

"I don't speak Arabic."

Noel wanted me along anyway, so once we boarded, I started spouting out names of Arab dishes to find common ground. In the meantime, Noel was trying to rip off the captain. Shots were fired. It all went so fast that, the next thing I remember, I was in the back of a car with Noel, speeding over a bridge that my father had recently paved.

The cops were waiting on the other side. But I was never charged. A Lebanese judge who knew my family phoned my father at home. Both thought it was a good idea to get me

In the drum and bugle corps. That's my younger brother, Wally, next to me. He got sent there for being a good guy. I got sent there for being a delinquent.

out of the city. So I was enrolled at King's College, a very blue-blood Anglo-Saxon boarding school, with one token Jew, one token Black and me, a Lebanese kid who refused to trim his Afro.

This was supposed to be a prestigious place. But when you'd get to talking to the other kids, you realized what a scam the administration was running on us. Rather than an institution of higher learning, King's College was a glorified reform school where rich parents could ship off their fucked-up kids. Having said that, it did straighten me, as well as many others, out in the long run. And it's now considered one of the best boarding schools of its kind. My schoolmates and I were a band of misfits — which helped prepare me for the literal band of misfits I'd join a few years later.

What I hated most about the school was the requirement that we go through military maneuvers. Why the fuck would I want to run around with a gun? That's why I was in trouble in the first place.

39

To avoid these stupid drills, I joined the band and played the snare drum. And that's where my drumming really began.

But I hadn't completely turned the corner. Noel Winters was still around. To an extent, he was the first rock star I ever knew. He couldn't play an instrument to save his life. But the chicks loved him, other guys loved him, even the cops who were trying to arrest him were taken in by his charisma.

Noel taught me that people were going to try to get over on me, and I'd better fight for what I wanted. When I'd get into trouble, he'd look me in the eye and ask, "Tom, did you really fuck up, or did you get fucked?" — a question I'd ponder quite a bit in the rock 'n' roll business. He explained that the code of ethics most of us were taught was flawed. Because sometimes when you do your best, you still get fucked. And sometimes when you do things wrong, you end up hitting it out of the park and everyone thinks you're a hero.

During the summer, Noel and I rode motorcycles with his hardcore biker friends. At one point, I got into an accident and lost the lateral meniscus in my left knee, while suffering a concussion and cracking my shoulder. For the month that I was in the hospital, Noel arrived like clockwork every Wednesday and Sunday, leaving two cold beers in the toilet tank. When the nurses asked me to walk, I'd say I was too sore. But Noel gave me incentive. Cold brew in a room with no air-conditioning got my ass across the floor faster than weeks of physical therapy ever could.

Noel had the same kind of charisma I'd discover in real celebrities later on. At the hospital, all the nurses were drawn to him. I remember two stunning candy stripers who hung around, too — one of whom was actually named Marilyn Munro. Before my release, I ended up making out with both of them.

I give all credit to Noel for this achievement.

Still, he was a bad influence. During a trip to Prince Edward Island, he pulled me into a brawl with a rival gang. It all started when we stole their motorcycle helmets. They had to buy football helmets before they could get on their bikes and track us down. It would

A few years later, with my lifelong friends the Morgan twins, Dave (left) and Steve.

have made a really funny sight, seeing these badass bikers with high school helmets, if they hadn't been so intent on killing us.

The next day, I ran into some educated buddies — the Morgans, a pair of twins who were my best "normal" friends, growing up — at a campground, hanging out with their ladies, having a lovely time. And I thought, *What the fuck am I doing with these crazy bikers? I should go to the university.*

And so I changed my focus and ended up accepted to King's College, part of Dalhousie University in Halifax, where I continued playing drums and, by my second year, was appointed chief of the campus police. I was still a little wild — you can't fight genetics — but I was learning how to function in society.

Sadly, Noel Winters never did. In 1984, some kids found the dismembered bodies of two bikers from Montreal in plastic bags at the Browns Flat dump in New Brunswick. By all accounts, they were trying to break into Noel's territory, and may have had plans to kill him. Instead, Noel got to them first, then shot their female companions because, after all, he couldn't leave any witnesses. Police tracked down one of Noel's friends, who led them to the place where he'd helped Noel bury his victims.

While Noel sat in a cell, police discovered more. In 1983, a father and son had helped Noel renovate his home. But after a little too much to drink afterwards, Noel became convinced that they were plotting his murder. So he blasted the father in the face with a shotgun and used a pistol to put a bullet through the son's head.

Noel had plenty of powerful friends and — as I'd experienced myself — had done people a lot of favors. But this time, no one stepped forward to help him. Facing life behind bars, he killed himself in prison.

I wish I'd been able to speak to Noel before he reached his irreversible decision. He'd been good to me, and maybe I could have convinced him that there was a reason to live. But the truth was that I'd moved on, and a crime is a crime.

Although he was one of the most loyal friends I ever had in my life, I was glad I got away from him. I still had my own demons to wrestle.

Even when I was at the university, it was all but preordained that I'd be going into the family business. When I finally did, though, my dad was in the process of drinking everything away. Eventually, he brought in some partners who, predictably, threw him out. They wanted me to stick around — and even dangled a promise about letting me run the Maritime region — but I couldn't do that to my father.

So I applied for graduate school and was accepted into the master's program for urban planning at York University in Toronto. My dad watched me pack up a U-Haul, and noticed that I was having a difficult time negotiating space. At one point, I couldn't decide whether to take along my drums or a wicker couch.

My father wandered over and looked from item to item.

"Take the drums," he said. "I think you're going to need them."

I was touched that he still wanted me to play — since I'd tormented him during his hangovers while bashing the drums to *In-A-Gadda-Da-Vida*.

It was either the best — or the worst — advice I'd ever receive.

CHAPTER
five ———————————————————

My girlfriend at the time decided to move to Toronto as well, and got a job as a waitress at a place called the El Mocambo Tavern, not far from Grossman's. It had been around since the 1940s. Previously, a music venue had opened at the same address in 1850, and was said to be a refuge for escaped slaves from the United States. In every way, the El Mocambo was a piece of living history. Over the years, lots of famous acts appeared on the stage, playing everything from jazz to punk: U2, Elvis Costello, Blondie, the Ramones, Jimi Hendrix, Charles Mingus, Grover Washington Jr. and Al Di Meola. Stevie Ray Vaughan's 1983 renditions of "Little Wing," "Texas Flood" and "Lenny" live at El Mocambo are part of international lore. Even Marilyn Monroe performed there.

In 1977, fans were invited to see a series of gigs by an unknown band called the Cockroaches. Those who turned up first watched Montreal-based April Wine warm up the crowd. Then the Cockroaches came out — and revealed themselves to be the Rolling Stones, playing their first live club date in 14 years. The highlights comprise one side of the Stones' double album *Love You Live*. Taking advantage of the sophisticated recording equipment that the Stones brought to the building, April Wine released a live album as well.

One day, my girlfriend asked me if I also wanted a job at El Mocambo. I showed up, expecting to be handed an apron. Instead, I was given a tie. "You're a little, stocky guy," I was told. "You're the doorman. If you get into a confrontation, make sure one of the bigger guys is standing behind you."

I lost my first fight to a girl who kicked me in the nuts and strangled me with my own tie. The big guy behind me, Keith, promptly pushed her down the stairs.

"You can't do that to a girl," I said.

"If she wants to act like a man, we'll treat her like one."

Every night, in addition to interacting with the customers, I was hanging out with the bands. At first, I was a little hesitant to describe myself to them as a drummer. After all, I wasn't exactly living the life; I'd come to Toronto to be a graduate student. But the music scene was so rich, I felt like I had to be a part of it.

Toronto was filled with great venues — the Big Smoke, X-Rays, Albert's Hall, the Horseshoe, Bluesville — and, no longer feeling the pressure to save my family's asphalt business, I was able to give in to this side of myself.

I had a cousin in Toronto, Dr. David "Slice" Stephen, who'd always come around, bugging me to play football with him and his friends in the medical profession. Then, when the games were over, he'd bring me to these jam sessions run by Hock Walsh, who along with his brother, Donnie "Mr. Downchild" Walsh, cofounded the Downchild Blues Band in 1969. It was one of the few Canadian bands devoted exclusively to the development of the blues. Despite this distinction, Hock and his brother are best remembered as the

At the Horseshoe in Toronto, reliving the Blues Brothers tradition.
John Candy on left, Dan Aykroyd on right, Jeff on guitar.

inspiration for Toronto native Dan Aykroyd's creation the Blues Brothers. Aykroyd's Elwood Blues was modeled after Donnie, while John Belushi's Jake Blues was patterned after Hock. Three songs featured on the first Blues Brothers' album — "Shotgun Blues," "I Got Everything I Need (Almost)" and "Flip, Flop and Fly" — appeared on the Downchild Blues Band's second LP, *Straight Up*. Belushi's version of "Flip, Flop and Fly," in particular, is sung in a distinct Hock Walsh style.

There's another parallel between Hock and John Belushi. Hock liked to party so hard that, on one occasion, he practically killed Jeff by plying him with cocaine.

At first, I attended these gatherings solely as a spectator. Hock sometimes ran the jam sessions with Danny Marks, a founding member of the group Edward Bear and host of the Canadian TV show *Stormy Monday* and CBC radio series *The Hum Line*. Danny took a lot of pride in bridging the divide between blues and pop, and generations of Canadian guitarists grew up practicing his covers of

"Every Day I Have the Blues" and "Hideaway." As a sideman, Danny worked with Bo Diddley, the Average White Band, Ronnie Hawkins and Rita Coolidge, among others. Danny was a smart guy who knew rock 'n' roll was a business and purchased real estate with his earnings. Because of this income source, he was able to devote even more time to music. Unfortunately, he was quite full of himself, and kind of a snob.

He was part of something called the Toronto Blues Society. Some of the members weren't even musicians — and, to be honest, barely rated as people. But man, that never prevented them from tarnishing anyone who didn't live up to their haughty expectations.

One day, Danny announced that one of his regular jam-session drummers was sick, and asked if anyone knew a good substitute. My cousin, Slice, piped up: "Tom will do it."

In the years since my time in Battery Operated Electric Cow, I'd developed a routine, going to the record store every Tuesday and purchasing a new single, then putting on my headphones at home and jamming along with the tune. The process gave me a real jam feel and the freedom to improvise — something that Jeff Healey would later find valuable when we jammed free-form.

I also had some experience playing alongside actual musicians. One summer, while working at a job inspecting gravel pits in Halifax, I joined a band that included a dog that barked on cue. We even got a job on a tourist boat — for all the food and booze we could consume. We were fired when the captain told us, "You guys drink so much, I can't afford you."

At the jam session, I remember watching Danny's squinty eyes following me as I sat down at the drum kit. As the music began, I saw Danny scrutinizing every beat. I thought I was doing a pretty decent job. But halfway through the first song, he waved his arms to stop the music.

"Get the fuck out of here," Danny snapped. "You're not a drummer."

I should have hated the guy. But, without realizing it, Danny did me a favor. Suddenly, drumming wasn't a joke to me anymore. By shutting me down, Danny taught me that I might have had the talent, but I didn't have the spark.

Now all I wanted to do was become a "real" goddamn drummer.

Not long afterwards, while Danny was off somewhere else, I was again given the opportunity to drum at one of the jams. Hock Walsh was in charge that day. And this time, I delivered. The next time Danny and I saw each other at a session, Hock wanted me there. Interestingly, Danny didn't protest. He listened. And apparently he liked what he heard. Because when the jam was over, he started acting like a nice guy.

If that didn't seal my place in the scene, Hock discovered that I owned a reel-to-reel recorder, which was a really huge deal at the time. At that stage, I went from being a hanger-on to an integral part of the group. If Hock was having a session, he specifically requested that I attend, too — as long as I brought my reel-to-reel.

As I was quick to learn, most of these blues guys were hustlers.

Michael Pickett, who sang and played harmonica for the bands Whiskey Howl and Wooden Teeth before establishing himself as a solo artist, called me one day, anxious to jam the next morning.

"Tomorrow *morning*?" I asked, a little confused. I knew that most professional musicians didn't usually wake up before 1 p.m.

"Yeah, Tom. Ten o'clock."

Well, if a guy as accomplished as Pickett wanted to jam that early, I was up for it. I was awake at eight, packed my drums and even brought over a case of beer.

Pickett was really happy to see the beer, since he was pretty hungover and needed something to help start his day. The only problem was that he didn't have time to jam.

He'd called me to help him move.

Honestly, I barely cared. Yes, Michael had taken advantage of me, but I was becoming a bigger part of his world than the one I'd moved to Toronto to pursue. In class at grad school, I'd be recreating the prior night's jam session in my head. Some of the musicians had horrible personal lives, but they were incredible players who could tap into a part of themselves that made the listener introspective.

I know that's the impact that they had on me.

At a typical jam, you'd wait your turn to play. If you were having a good day, you might play three songs. If you were off, you'd be limited to one. Regardless, you were learning something every time — and meeting the important players on the scene.

By becoming a regular at these jam sessions, I eventually crossed paths with Buzz Upshaw, the garbage man with one leg shorter than the other. "You're not a bad drummer," he told me. "You've got some issues with timing. But we can work on that. I'd really like it if you were in my band."

That was quite an honor. Buzz was the real deal. And he wanted me not so he could use my gear, but because he liked my playing.

I credit Buzz with giving me the education that prepared me for my time with Jeff. He taught me about the need to follow the guitar players when I drummed — following the game plan, following the music, following the breaks, bringing up the volume when the situation called for it, then taking it down. As a free-form player, Buzz was more regimented than Jeff, and helped me develop the skills I'd need to become a professional. It was Buzz who introduced me to musicians like bassist Gary Latimer and saxophonist Wimpy Zankowski, excellent players with whom I'd graduate from jam sessions to money gigs.

Despite all this, Buzz wasn't really accepted by the blues community. I think it had a lot to do with his peculiar habits, including a tendency to fall asleep in the middle of conversations. For weeks, we were trying to get a gig at the Chick'N'Deli, which, despite the name, was a gathering place for some of the top musicians in the city. But we couldn't track down the booker, a real old-school guy who liked to tell stories about hanging with Sinatra and other giants of that era. Buzz and I were in a van one night, pulling a trailer, talking about our strategy, when he suddenly dozed off, clipped a pedestrian and spun him around. Fortunately, we were going slow. The guy wasn't hurt, just pissed off. He was standing there in the street, screaming, when Buzz looked through the rearview mirror and got very excited.

"Hey, Tom. That's the guy from the Chick'N'Deli. He's waving at us. Let's get out and ask him for a gig."

"He's not waving at us. He's yelling at us. You just nearly killed him, Buzz. Let's get the fuck out of here."

Buzz listened to me. Because he was a big teddy bear and didn't have a lot of ambition, he was very comfortable allowing me to make decisions on behalf of the band. As we raised our profile, I became the group's de facto manager, booking our dates, putting together our schedule, negotiating fees, paying the band. All musicians claim that they want to earn a living from their craft. But what I learned early was that getting them to all show up at the same place at the same time was an art in itself.

I was keeping musician's hours, even though I was in graduate school, but I wasn't alone. Sometimes, I'd be staggering to school in the morning — after playing all night at a booze-can, the local term for an after-hours joint — and another guy from the scene would pass me in his bread truck, pull over to the side, offer me a lift and hand me a couple of fresh rolls.

After one show, Buzz and I decided to leave our gear in a club and come back later to pick it up. When we returned, though, we discovered that our shit was stolen. I remembered the same thing happening to my father's crews on construction sites — when bulldozers, trucks and rollers would go missing — and knew that, if I asked around, I'd find our stuff. The scene was small, and when you're a thief who comes across that kind of a stash, it's hard to keep your mouth shut. It took a few weeks, but after I talked to a guy who talked to a guy who talked to a guy who talked to the thief, we got everything back — without calling the cops or throwing a punch.

I was applying the skills I knew to the craft I loved. I hadn't been in the scene as long as everybody else, but I'd already become adept at navigating the territory.

CHAPTER
six

Jeff Healey was master of his scene. If there was any discomfort that he felt as a blind man, an outsider wouldn't have noticed. Even in his teens, he felt that he didn't have to prove himself to the Blues Society types and jazz snobs. It was Jeff's world. He was the commander. There could be two hundred other people in the room, but Jeff was calling the shots.

Sometimes I think about how my life would have turned out if Buzz Upshaw hadn't invited me to join his band. Jeff may have never heard me play, and I might have proceeded with my strategy to become an urban planner. By the time I finished grad school in 1984, I was already playing with Jeff and had an office job in downtown Toronto. I knew that I couldn't live in both worlds. But if I'd never gotten any further than Buzz Upshaw's band, I might have had no choice but to stay in the field that I'd studied.

Backing up my musical mentor, Buzz Upshaw.

So I want to give all credit to Buzz here. The man was world class. Unfortunately, he didn't live long enough to get his pension. And there's a lesson there, too. Don't compromise on your dreams. You don't know how long you'll be here.

Or, as we said in one of the Jeff Healey Band's songs, "It could all get blown away."

Of course, musicians are competitive people, and the fact that I did have a fallback option was a source of jealousy in some cases, and condescension in others. "He's not a real drummer," I'd hear. "He's an urban planner." I always tried to act tough, but we're all sensitive at our core. I'd never let my detractors realize that their words stung, but since I'm telling the truth right now, I'll give them the satisfaction of knowing that these comments bugged the hell out of me.

When Jeff first told me he was blind, I thought he was having a laugh at my expense. Jeff's humor didn't always hit you over the head. He was cerebral, and he liked to keep you guessing about whether he was joking or not. But then I noticed that when he moved around, he'd bump into a lot of things. Very rarely did he ever reach out his arm for assistance. Because he was such an integral part of the scene, a lot of his friends, and some of their girlfriends, would always be conscious of Jeff, in case he suddenly needed help.

These weren't necessarily the kindest people in the world. Yet they could feel Jeff's magic and wanted to be near it, as if some of the greatness might extend to them. Onstage, Jeff could stretch octaves. No one can do that. He jammed with both his left and right hands — more aggressively than anyone I've ever seen. But what really blew everyone's mind was when Jeff would leap out of his chair, holding that guitar against his leg with no guitar strap and jump all over the goddamn place, blasting out these notes. In theory, this should have been impossible. There was nothing else like it.

When I was still in Buzz's band, I noticed that, as the weeks passed, Jeff was sitting in with us with greater frequency. After his storied jam sessions with Albert Collins, I heard, Grossman's was besieged by booking agents. But Jeff didn't have an official group. "Most of the bands that were forming didn't want me around," he said in one interview, "because they figured that, just from my playing style — holding the guitar the way I do — that I would be sort of the oddball. Everyone would be watching me. I've never tried lifting my guitar and playing it conventionally. I can play a few chords that way, but I can't play a lead to save my life.

"So everyone would wish me a lot of luck and say that, if I kept at it, I'd go far. But I was thinking, 'I love to play music, but possibly I'm not cut out for this.' I was thinking about maybe going into broadcasting as an engineer or something."

Jeff was probably exaggerating his lack of musical prospects. Certainly there were musicians who didn't want him in their bands. But that was likely because they were too insecure to be upstaged.

And others — Jeff would never admit to the media — were too far below his standard. Despite my lack of experience, though, he appeared to like playing with me. After a while, he urged me to take some gigs with him when I wasn't busy with Buzz.

I'd always run it by Buzz, out of respect: "Look. This guy Healey wants me to play at his gig next Wednesday. Are you cool with that?" Invariably, he was.

During one of our first jams, we were playing with this killer bassist named Terry. Jeff was ripping out these solos, the band was starting to cook and I could feel everything building. *Ten, nine, eight . . .*

Terry had smoked a big doobie before the show and wasn't prepared when Jeff rocketed out of his chair. The look of shock was something to see, as Jeff tore into the audience, playing the guitar hard against his thighs, toppling tables and chairs and patrons. He hoisted his guitar over his head, played with his teeth, whirled all over the place. Then, with nobody's help, he found his way back to his chair.

"Thank you very much," he said politely, ending the performance. "See you all again soon."

I was blown away by Jeff's crazy antics. But what lingered with me was the expression on Terry's face: *What the fuck have I been smoking?* In the years to come, I'd see the greatest musicians in the world react the exact same way.

After a while, my relationship with Jeff progressed. He asked me to be his first-call drummer — meaning that, if I wasn't with Buzz, I was with him. Not only did I agree, but I committed myself to finding the substitutes for those nights when I wasn't around.

After I made the decision to officially join Jeff's band, I felt like I'd been handed a gift. Buzz and I were able to remain friends because I wasn't the greatest blues drummer, and he had plenty of other choices on the scene. I played better with Jeff because of his free-form style. I'd never really had formal lessons — with the exception of some coaching from a drum teacher in Saint John named Peter Conway, I learned to play in my room while listening to the Who and other rock bands — so I guess I was free-form, too. And Jeff was able to feed off of that. Even Buzz acknowledged it.

We had a really solid bass player at the time, but like many musicians, he wasn't that reliable. Neither Jeff nor I could take a risk with someone who could sabotage us because we were never sure whether he'd have his bass around his shoulders when the lights went on. After I met Joe Rockman, my instincts told me that he'd be a better fit.

When Joe was eight, he began studying classical piano at the Royal Conservatory of Music. At 12, he switched to classical guitar for another six years until deciding that he wanted to play the bass. He'd been working as a successful session musician when the three of us first played together at Grossman's one Sunday night in 1985. "Within 16 bars," Joe told *Canadian Musician* magazine, "we established a musical connection that is rare. It was like electric shock. I knew that the three of us together could be very, very big."

So immediate was the bond we all felt that Joe severed ties with his various clients, cutting his salary down to something in the neighborhood of fifty Canadian dollars a week. He said that the mentality in the studio was completely different than what we experienced onstage, and that he suspected he'd never have the chance to meet up with a musician of Jeff's caliber again.

When the three of us were playing, Joe was responsible for keeping the time and anchoring the harmonic movement, holding the notes for long stretches so Jeff and I could improvise and fill in the spaces. "We seemed to be able to pick where the others would come in," Jeff described our onstage chemistry to England's *Guitarist* magazine in 1989. "Tom would pick up where Joe left something out, and so on . . . It worked, and so we never saw any reason to change it."

When our first session ended, the three of us came offstage and shook hands.

"Okay, it's a band," Jeff announced. "Let's go to work."

After that, there were only two gigs — out of hundreds — that we ever missed. The first time was in my hometown: some of my friends got Jeff too drunk to play. After we sobered him up for hours, he still managed to play five songs, which was no concert, as far as any of us were concerned. The second time, we were in Scotland, and he had a terrible sore throat. Jeff couldn't talk but still insisted on going onstage. But the doctor said, "No way."

Each of us played a specific and vital role in the group. It goes without saying that Jeff was born blessed with abilities few humans will ever possess. While I struggled to become the kind of drummer who could dignify an artist like Jeff Healey, Jeff barely practiced. "I'm probably the world's worst practicer," he admitted to *Guitar Player* magazine. "I never liked it. I never liked the word 'practice,' which is why I quit taking piano lessons, and I never really practiced guitar. My practice came from sitting with a bunch of people, or sitting by myself with records, playing along with somebody's solo . . . and then starting to work my own ideas into that."

Jeff didn't just imitate the sounds he heard on guitar solos. He carefully studied the keyboard, saxophone and trumpet parts of the songs he liked. "You just learn so much more music that way," he said, "and that's how the evolution of music happens."

For whatever reason — let's say destiny, for lack of a better word — he was able to go from sitting alone in his room to getting his talent out in front of people. I credit myself with being the guy who largely helped him do it, even if it meant clashing with him and much of the industry to realize our vision. Joe was not just the man in the middle but also the caretaker and peacemaker. When we started expanding our fan base, Joe made sure we consistently responded to our supporters and maintained their loyalty. And Joe and Jeff were very close. Onstage, Jeff instinctively turned to Joe, almost for his guidance. If Jeff was positioned in the wrong place, he'd allow Joe to gently bump him toward the proper spot. No one else could do that. But Jeff trusted Joe in a unique way.

Could Jeff have found better musicians? Maybe. But an agent once told me that he'd seen a lot of acts comprised of top-level players who, cumulatively, couldn't excite the crowd. Joe and I were able to bring something out in Jeff that others couldn't. As great as Jeff was as a musician, I'm not sure how he'd be remembered if the three of us hadn't been a team.

Emotionally, we all had our issues. Jeff had been adopted, and didn't know where he came from before the Healeys welcomed him into their family. Joe was dealing with his own insecurities. I was the product of divorce, alcoholism and general dysfunction. Each one of us shared the same feeling of longing and desperately needed to fill the gaps.

Jeff and I were playing with lyrics one night and came up with two lines that never turned into a song. Still, it expresses the way we both viewed the world:

My heart is broken in so many places
Not enough love to fill all the spaces

When we confided to each other, we all had the same story about our early romances: pining for the girl who didn't know we existed. Then, suddenly, these three awkward guys were fending off two or three girls a day. This wasn't necessarily good. When you go from zero to one hundred with no transition, you lack the emotional maturity to deal with your new circumstances — the same as people who win the lottery and blow all their cash. I think we were all trying to fill the voids in our lives, and make up for lost time. And even though we agreed that certain women were off-limits, we didn't necessarily live by our rules. If you look through the annals of rock 'n' roll, that's a common theme. When someone in the band has a new girl, suddenly everyone's checking her out — including the roadies.

Sometimes Jeff described the holes in our lives as places where demons hid. But the demons didn't come from the outside. They came from within us, and we filled the voids with girls, drugs and booze. On occasion, though, we got it right and filled it with music.

Those were the times when the band got to soar with the gods.

On those nights when we were all cooking onstage, Jeff told me he felt like he was touching places that no one else could reach.

"It's the one time you know who you are, where you are and what you are," he said, "and what you're meant to be."

As we fantasized about our own rock 'n' roll future, we studied Jeff's record collection. Every time we listened to a song — on a gramophone he'd altered so he could play his music with ease — I felt like I was taking a college course. Robert Johnson, Jeff explained, was one of the first slide specialists, along with Son House and lesser-known musicians like Kokomo Arnold.

I can't even describe what it was like to have access to all this music — years before iTunes and the internet. I saw one article claiming that Jeff had twenty-five thousand discs at home. I think the actual number exceeded a hundred thousand. Later, when we became well known, he'd show off the collection to reporters. One of his favorite tricks was telling the guy, "Hey, you have to hear this record." Then he'd walk over to the wall and pull it out. Without exception, the reporters wrote about the blind singer who knew where every one of his records was located.

Once the fans realized that Jeff was a collector, they'd bring him old 78s. I'd watch him visit people's homes and go through their records in the living room. Generally, he'd find only three or four that he thought were acceptable. The rest were left in a pile of discards.

We were listening to music one night — and smoking a lot of hash — when Jeff proclaimed, "I like this sound. It sounds blue to me. When I play my old records, they sound blue."

"But you're blind," I said. "How can you know what blue even looks like?"

"It's one of the sounds in my head. It's like when we're jamming out and doubling the tempo, the sound in my head is red."

I was too stoned to really grasp what he was saying. When I looked over at Jeff, he was twirling his hair and smiling at me. I tried to bring up this topic again at other times, but could never really get the right words out. To this day, I'm not sure if Jeff really "heard" colors or was just fucking with me.

The guy just had so much depth. When I looked at Jeff's records, I imagined his name under the corporate logo. It would make me angry, thinking about all those labels that had passed on him. Maybe the Canadians were too small-minded, I concluded. Eventually we'd end up in the United States and make those executives regret ever dismissing Jeff as a "gimmick."

Every time one of the blues greats came to town, he'd seek Jeff out — without exception. If these guys knew Jeff's value, I predicted, so would everybody else. Even at 19 years old, Jeff had a solid ego and knew where he belonged. The challenge was getting there.

But if I was giving up my urban planning gig, I was going to go all the way. Jeff had another manager at the time — Corey, the photographer, who'd promoted him locally — and I made no secret of the fact that I wanted to get involved in the business of the band.

Corey was a gentle soul who didn't have the killer instinct or the vision to take the Jeff Healey Band out of familiar territory. "If you can get the band a contract," he told me with gracious sincerity, "I'll step aside."

I was nervous about calling my mother to tell her about my change in life plans. In a Lebanese family, you're not supposed to go all the way through graduate school then try to become a musician instead. "Ma, I met this guy, Jeff, and I'm going to make him a famous guitarist, and we're going to travel all over the world." She could tell I'd had a few drinks. "That's nice, dear," she said. "Now, get some sleep." But she later told me that there was something in my voice that convinced her that our rock 'n' roll dreams were really going to happen.

Because of Jeff's age, I also wanted to talk to his father. Jeff resisted this. "I make my own calls," he argued.

"I understand. But you're young and there's nothing wrong with your parents worrying about what we're thinking about. I'm not seeing Ontario or even just Canada here. I'm talking about getting on planes for gigs in America, Europe, Japan, Australia." I had no idea how I would pull this off, but in my heart I knew that Jeff could not be denied.

Jeff's parents didn't really care about fame. Even when we had it, you'd never see them parading through hotel lobbies in Jeff Healey hats and jackets so the other guests would know that their kid was a star. They simply enjoyed coming to the gigs and listening to him do what he loved. Even though they'd raised Jeff to be independent, they were concerned about his disability and how the type of plan I was advocating would impact him. But they also knew that it would have been a crime to contain his talent. So when I discussed our goals with Bud Healey, he gave me his blessing.

As time went on, I'd wonder whether he ever questioned his decision. But despite all the tribulations that the Jeff Healey Band would endure, I hope Bud understood that my heart was in the right place.

seven

One of the first things I noticed was that, whenever we played a bar or a nightclub, the price of drinks was immediately marked up — from 100 to 300 percent. The Jeff Healey Band had a pretty good following at this point, and our friends and fans tended to be drinkers. If we had three hundred people in the room, the club was making an extra couple of thousand dollars, even after we got paid.

I knew we weren't in a position to ask for a percentage of liquor sales. But when people came to see us, there was always a cover charge. If the bar could profit from the increased bar tab, we deserved to make money from the door. As Jeff put it, "Why should someone else take in the gravy after we've done all the work?"

At first, when I brought this topic up, I expected the bar owners to hesitate. But they didn't. It taught me an important lesson.

Playing the Misty Moon in Halifax — just prior to my first cocaine party.

Sometimes you only go as far as you allow yourself. Had I not said anything, no one would have offered us an extra dime. But they didn't want to piss us off, either, and lose us to another club. So eventually our arrangement was that we'd play for the door.

Being up onstage with a guy as talented as Jeff, seeing the crowds grow with each passing week, feeling the momentum going forward, was exciting. To this day, I believe that playing a hot club is the best gig in the world for a live band. It's not exactly a tough job — doing something creative, drinking free booze and having lovely ladies show overwhelming interest in you. Not bad for three misfits who'd never otherwise have been in that position unless we launched a successful computer company or something.

Without the internet, a lot of our reputation came from word of mouth. That was how we got booked for a gig in Nova Scotia. At a party afterwards, I saw Jeff doing coke with the host. Believe it or not, I'd never tried it before. But if I was going to be a rock star, I figured, it was time to start. Eventually I was so blitzed that I fell asleep on the couch. With my eyes closed, I reached for what I thought was a pillow. It was really a large ashtray. I woke up with ashes in my nose and mouth.

Previously, I'd occasionally grub a cigarette from Jeff. But when Jeff lit up the next morning, I grabbed the butt out of his mouth and tossed it away. I never smoked again. The smell made me nauseous. Unfortunately, I couldn't say the same about cocaine.

As I was researching this book, one of the most touching things I heard came from Gary Scrutton, a roadie who remembered that, as much as we liked to party, Joe and I always looked out for Jeff first. We'd let loose with abandon as long as we knew that he was being taken care of. I recall watching Joe onstage at a gig at Queen's University in Kingston, Ontario, when suddenly some small item flew right by him, in Jeff's direction. Joe immediately put down his bass and went after some guy in the crowd. By the time I got around my drums, the bouncers had grabbed the dude and were pulling him away. It turned out that he'd been flicking beer caps at Jeff. Nothing hit him, but Joe was not going to take any chances. Our philosophy was: Protect Jeff. Protect the band. Stick together.

It was a good time in our lives. I'd be sitting behind the drums and spot a reporter or photographer in the crowd and know that our reputation was building. Even with all the bullshit that would transpire between the band members in the years to come, there's very little that I'd change.

Where I came from, you had to join the navy to see the world. We were going to take this band everywhere. I was sure of it.

Other artists in our position were dependent on an agent, who had to be convinced to get them bookings. If the agent actually did his job, he'd cut a deal with an entertainment venue and take a commission in the process. Whatever was left went to the musicians, who were relentlessly reminded how lucky they were to have an agent who parted the heavens to get them the gig.

The strategy had nothing to do with career-building. It had to do with the relationship between the club and the agent. From working

Jeff tries Lebanese cuisine during a visit with my brother, Wally, in Halifax.

at Stephen Construction with my family, I understood business, and knew that we deserved — and could do — better. So did Jeff. "It's pretty hard to get to the moon," he said, "when other people want you to howl at it."

The question we started asking was, "Does this make sense for us?" Our motive wasn't solely making a profit, although that was a definite factor; it was building the Jeff Healey Band's reputation — or brand, as we'd say today.

Our first step was getting out of Ontario. Because of the audience we were drawing in Toronto, clubs all over Canada were anxious to have us. So we hit the road. A lot of the places were absolute dives. But that never stopped the people from coming to see us.

Sometimes it was so cold that snow was blowing through the cracks in the hotel windows. You'd go out to get a cup of coffee and sink up to your waist in snow. Still, we were having a blast. We were learning every time we played. We adjusted to crowds with different tastes. The band was cooking. We were best friends. And every single one of us wanted to be at our gigs.

As everyone knew, Jeff's inspiration came from a place no one else could see. As a result, he'd always been an uninhibited presence onstage. But as we toured, he became even more of a showman, running through the crowd as the audience jumped out of his way, laughing and screaming. When Bud Healey eventually saw this side of his son, he responded with a mixture of bafflement and consternation.

"That's a needless thing to do," Bud said, perhaps believing that Jeff had so much innate talent that it was unnecessary to accessorize his performances.

Yet, almost without exception, the media picked up on Jeff's antics and made it sound like skipping a Jeff Healey Band gig was equivalent to missing a Beatles performance circa 1962.

It was an exaggeration, of course, but, man, we put on a pretty good show. Sometimes, Jeff would place his guitar on the stage and stand on the whammy bar and start dancing. Given his size, you'd think that the guitar would be destroyed. But he was delicate enough to apply just enough pressure to make interesting sounds.

Jeff was doing a solo during our "All Along the Watchtower" cover one time when, unexpectedly, he began hammering his guitar on the ground. The thing splintered, with one part hitting a chair and another part clanging against my bass drum. The body was still on the stage, though, and — even though he was blind — Jeff knew exactly where it was. Stepping onto the whammy bar, he did his thing, then walked off the stage.

When I went to the dressing room afterwards, Jeff was smoking a cigarette, twirling his hair and smiling. "Fuck," I said, "we just bought that guitar. That's a lot of money. But, man, that was great."

"The second part's right," Jeff smirked. In other words, he was a showman — like Pete Townshend or Jimi Hendrix — and the cost of a smashed instrument was not his concern.

Because we didn't have an unlimited budget, our roadie, Gary Scrutton, began patching up Jeff's guitar night after night. It was a reverse of the Humpty Dumpty rhyme. Maybe all the king's horses and all the king's men couldn't put Humpty Dumpty back together again, but Gary Scrutton probably could.

During one show, Jeff was playing the way he normally did, with his guitar in his lap. Then, out of nowhere, he leaped up, banged his head on the ceiling and, without missing a beat, began picking at the guitar with his teeth — playing beautiful chords.

Today, you can still find the interview Jeff did with David Letterman, describing his penchant for scratching his enamel against the guitar strings. "My dentist doesn't like it at all," he cracked to the talk show host. The audience responded with laughter and applause. I was equally amused — even though I'd heard him deliver that line dozens of times before.

In time, we built a little stand for Jeff in case he felt like playing standing up. "Tom and I would look out into the audience and notice that, when people in the front row were standing, they were the only ones who could properly see Jeff," Joe recalled in our fan bulletin. "So we sat down with Jeff and our guitar technician and put together our ideas, which later turned into the stand . . . It had to be designed so that Jeff would be comfortable and able to angle his wrists properly. Also, it needed to . . . come apart for the spots in the show when Jeff wanted to be seated . . . It certainly allows Jeff to stretch out his 6'2" frame."

The more we traveled, the more the local media was drawn to us — or, more specifically, to Jeff. Sure, the Jeff Healey Band consisted of three equal members. But let's be honest. If you're the host of a radio show, you really want to talk to the front man. And our front man was a little bit more interesting, and media savvy, than most others. On the air, the DJs would mention Joe and I, tell us they were happy we were alive but that, without Jeff, we wouldn't have gotten in the door.

Interestingly, it was Jeff who always insisted that Joe and I tag along, and would remind the media — at that stage, anyway — that we were a band.

"You know," Jeff told me one day, "I take a lot of shit for having you in the group."

Innocent and happy.

"Oh, yeah? What kind of shit?"

"People say you're a camel jockey, a terrorist, a Christ killer."

"Christ killer? Maybe they're talking about Joe."

We all had a good laugh. We were the ultimate trio of misfits: a blind guitarist, backed by a Lebo on drums and a Jew on bass.

"Oh," Jeff assured me, "they say stuff about Joe, too." Then he grinned. "But some of the jokes I heard are pretty good."

I was feeling defensive. "Like what?"

"Well, why can't the Lebanese play hockey?"

I waited for the punch line.

"Because every time they go around the corners, they open up a grocery store." Now that *was* funny.

Perhaps the best thing about being a musician is that it's the great equalizer. You can meet every type of human being and find a way to relate, because everybody loves music. It doesn't matter if you're talking to a movie star or the kid serving you pizza, or even if there's a language barrier. Once you get up on the stage, you have the ability to transcend everything. And because you're interacting with so many kinds of people, you subconsciously become more knowledgeable of lifestyles you might not have ever encountered and, subsequently, more tolerant.

Of course, you also have to deal with musicians. And that means that you often have to stare some sad cases in the face. Since the profession allows you to live like you're 18, you run into guys who seem to be waiting for their parents to get them out of their next jam. The problem is that, sometimes, these guys are in their fifties, and their parents are dead. So I'd be awestruck by some of the great players I'd watch in a club, then learn that they couldn't manage to buy a bag of groceries or pay their rent. And if they couldn't find a new girlfriend to take care of the bills, they might start asking you.

Without realizing it, we were developing many of the same disorders as these tragic figures, consuming alcohol and drugs in greater amounts. Sometimes, I'd complain that Jeff was partying too much. Then I'd hear that he said the exact same thing about me. Although never as prominent a part of the Jeff Healey Band as our playing, the booze became a bigger factor than the sex. After all, the groupies were not with us onstage. The vodka, rum, and Jack Daniel's were.

I was becoming a rum guy. Joe preferred rye. And Jeff — who barely tolerated beer — considered vodka his favorite drink.

"Hi, I'm Jeff Healey of the Jeff Healey Band," he'd announce in Winnipeg, Saskatoon or Moncton. "Please don't drink and drive. I know I don't."

As crazy as it seems, I knew he was lying.

The line got a good laugh among the audience members aware of Jeff's disability. As I said before, though, many didn't know that he was blind until we left town and they read an article about our performance in the paper. Even we forgot sometimes.

"I remember Jeff had moved into a new place, and I asked him, 'How's the apartment?'" says super-agent Ralph James. "Other people would talk about the view, the architecture, the way the sunlight shined through the windows. Jeff just said, 'It has great heat.'"

I have to admit that there were moments when it looked like Jeff was about to step in front of a truck, and I'd have to pull him back. In Edmonton once, when he was smashed, he walked up the escalator the wrong way, and took a bit of a fall. Joe and I managed to grab him before he broke any bones or hit his head, and carry him up the right escalator — while all three of us laughed like we were insane.

But for every story like this, there were just as many times when Jeff stepped forward to save my ass. So I don't know what's worse: being blind, being drunk or being blind drunk.

When I made my return to Halifax, where I attended college, all of my friends wanted to meet Jeff. One guy, a fraternity friend of mine, was so excited that he asked to go out with him alone. The next morning, he called me, sounding a little distressed.

"I don't know how to say this. But Jeff kind of smashed my car up?"

"What the fuck are you talking about?"

"We had a few drinks, and he wanted to drive."

I'd later discover that this was Jeff's MO. "And you let him?"

"I didn't see the harm in it. He's so good at everything else. But then he drove into this guy."

At this point, my heart jumped. If Jeff ran someone over, our career would be dead before it started. But my friend quickly assured me that Jeff simply collided with another car and no one was hurt.

There was more to the story, too. When the police arrived at the scene, they asked Jeff for his license.

"I don't have one," he explained.

"You mean, you don't *have* a driver's license, or you forgot to take it with you before you decided to get drunk and put yourself behind the wheel of a car?"

"I don't have one at all. I'm blind."

Fortunately for everyone involved, the officer had heard about the Jeff Healey Band through the local media and people who'd seen us play live. Instead of arresting his ass, he settled for an autograph. Shades of things to come.

On the tour bus, we alleviated the boredom by playing cards — sometimes for hours. Jeff was always in the middle of the game, playing with what I eventually realized was a braille deck. Not only could he read the cards with his fingers, he bent them a certain way to make them more identifiable. Then, one night, I realized that I could see the reflection of Jeff's cards in the window behind him, and started taking some of my money back.

"I don't know what you're doing, Tom," he promised. "But I'll figure it out."

Those were the moments I'd cling to later — the time when the bantering was good-natured, and the Jeff Healey Band was a brotherhood.

We were making money — not exorbitant amounts, but enough, considering that we were still unsigned. And so we made another radical decision. Since the groupies, the booze and the drugs were coming for free, we felt that we could begin saving dough and accumulate a war chest. Who ever heard of a rock 'n' roll band in our position with a bank account? But this way, when we wanted to make our next move, we had the capital to accomplish our goal.

So many other musicians would have taken whatever they'd earned and purchased a new amp. We had a better idea — let the *venue* supply the amp. That way, we could actually fly to some of our faraway gigs.

When I packed, I brought my snare drum and my favorite sticks. If the club owners wanted the Jeff Healey Band as much as they said they did, they'd make sure that we all had the gear we liked. Once we figured this out, we saved thousands of dollars, enabling us to fly many times instead of driving.

It was all fresh and fun. We toured Newfoundland in the summer, when it was absolutely beautiful. Jeff loved the Newfoundlanders and loved their accents, imitating them onstage.

"Lord tundering Jesus bye."

Normally, you'd get punched in the face for making fun of the Newfies. But when Jeff did it, they were delighted. Once again, he could do anything he wanted.

After a gig during the Newfoundland tour, we returned to the band house that the club provided. The place was a dump, with graffiti all over the walls, cigarette burns on the furniture and stains on the rug. Somehow, Jeff found a collection of milk cartons packed with old 78s. Feeling around the grooves, he'd stop when he found something that he thought might be a diamond in the bunch.

"Tom," he'd ask. "Does this label say Decca or Bluebird?"

I think he found two records he wanted that night. The rest, he determined, were shit.

When the sun came up, I heard something smashing outside and opened the door to investigate. Jeff was with two Newfoundlanders, winging records down the hill in front of the band house. One of the discs did a U-turn and went crashing through our window.

A neighbor, a female probably in her early twenties, swung open her door to scold us. Then she stopped and smiled. "Oh? Jeff Healey."

As with the girls, there was a danger to this type of indulgence. Jeff's secret pleasure was pushing people as far as he could and getting away with it. And these stunts reinforced his belief that he could get away with almost anything.

But I was as guilty of allowing that as anyone else. He just impressed the hell out of me, and I guess we were all pushing the limits.

• •

We were in northern Maine, not far from the Canadian border, when a blizzard hit. We were already set up and ready to play, but I was prepared to tell the club manager, "Just pay us half. We'll cancel the show and come back another time." Jeff wouldn't allow it. "There's two people out there who came to see us play," he argued. "A show's a show."

He had the same attitude about autographs. If fans were going to wait around to ask for his signature, Jeff would not leave until he signed, even if the process took hours.

I estimate that we played about 250 gigs a year during this period. It wasn't until we had a deal and were making money that we knew it was a hump. We didn't understand that all that traveling would wear us down.

At this point, Jeff and I were generally in synch mentally. We spent a lot of time together touring, and I learned a lot about him. He was uncomfortable around animals, particularly birds. One flew into him when he was a kid and clipped him with its sharp beak. Jeff was generally confident about most things that he'd encounter on the ground. But because birds swooped out of the air, he could never sense when one was coming.

During a swing through Alberta, we arrived back at the hotel at daybreak. Just after I fell asleep, Jeff called my room, more frantic than usual. A group of birds had congregated outside his window, and whenever he heard the *tweet, tweet, tweet*, he'd jump out of bed.

It was rare that Jeff asked for my assistance. It took a lot for him to reveal this vulnerability, and I couldn't let him down. Storming into the room, I pulled open the window and screamed, "Fuck off, birds!" Then I slammed the window shut so we could all sleep in peace.

As silly as it sounds, the birds actually listened to me. For years, Jeff would retell the story. When a crowd was being particularly obnoxious, we'd all laugh and yell, "Fuck off, birds!"

Jeff also hated fish. This had nothing to do with a childhood trauma. He just couldn't stand the smell. But during a visit to Kootenay Lake, surrounded by the exquisite Kokanee Range in the interior of British Columbia, we were all in a speedboat. Since there wasn't anything in our path, we felt comfortable with Jeff taking the wheel — even as we accelerated up to 45 miles an hour. After he got that out of his system, we stopped at a large houseboat, where a bunch of guys were fishing. Given Jeff's aversion, I thought he'd retreat to the cabin. Then he realized that no one was catching anything, and he wanted to try.

One of the fishermen eventually snared eight fish. But Jeff didn't stop until he'd captured 10. And that night, he even had a couple of bites of fish. He was so competitive that he was willing to forget his revulsion — and celebrate the fact that he'd won.

Still, all three of us knew that we wouldn't be able to label ourselves winners until we had a record deal. As much as I love Canada, I believe that the record company executives who'd previously rejected Jeff were parochial morons. And their hesitance was a stain on the country. How could they miss a kid who'd been on Canadian radio and television most of his life? It's not like he was hiding from anybody.

We were determined to show the world that there was a different kind of Canadian — and we'd prove it by managing the Jeff Healey Band ourselves.

To this day, people tell me that I should have focused on being a manager only or hired someone with a track record in the industry. But I couldn't. If a guy with Jeff's ability was still unsigned, then these great managers missed him. I enjoyed playing too much. And at the time, we didn't have other distractions, like most managers. So all three of us were 100 percent invested in our future.

Technically, we were equal partners; every decision that we made had to be unanimous. It was Jeff, Joe and Tom against the world. On paper, Jeff was the chairman, I was the president and Joe was the company's secretary-treasurer, encouraging me to raise the fee for our gigs and collect all the money that we were due.

"Tom was incredibly driven and tough, exceptionally shrewd, and also impatient and pushy," remembers Ben Richardson, who played bass for one of our opening bands, the Phantoms, and worked as our tour manager during two different periods. "He wasn't interested at all in settling down. He was interested in lots of partying, and making lots of money. But it was more of a game to him, the thrill of the chase. He believed that there was nothing that he couldn't do.

"He relentlessly hounded the press to write about the band, and scored a real coup when the *Globe and Mail* featured them on the front page of the entertainment section. Tom had that front page printed on high gloss paper at full size, and used it as the centerpiece of their promo kit, to badger club owners into hiring the band for escalating guarantees. But he also loved to play drums, and could've been a much better drummer if his life hadn't been consumed with business."

Bruce Allen, one of the great music managers, once told me, "Hey, Tom, you have to pick a team. You can't be on both sides at once. It's like being shirts and skins at the same time. Fuckin' impossible. How can you be the drunken drummer one night, keeping the band up until seven in the morning, then give them hell the next day for partying too much? It just won't work."

I remember consulting Tony Tobias, a family friend and industry veteran, and questioning him about our strategy. "Am I doing things right?" I said.

"No. But don't change. If it were me, I'd be doing things the way they've always been done, stumbling around like an idiot. You're breaking the rules, and it seems to be working for you."

To be honest, Jeff also had a selfish motive for embracing our management scheme. With Joe and I, Jeff could always control management. A heavyweight like Bruce Allen, for example, might not always be in the mood to take Jeff's shit. His bandmates, on the other hand, were willing to do whatever it took to make Jeff happy.

Remembers Thom Panunzio, the music heavyweight whose studio work with John Lennon, Bob Dylan, Bruce Springsteen, U2 and others has netted him more than 50 gold and platinum records, "Tom and Joe were really like Jeff's brothers. They looked after him. They loved him. They took care of him. Both of those guys really dedicated their lives to him, to the band, to the music — but also taking care of Jeff. There was nothing they wouldn't do for him. It was the Jeff Healey Band. He was the center of the show, and they protected him."

But I'd earned the disdain of a number of people who knew Jeff before I did. "There was a lot of backlash directed against Tom," Ben Richardson says. "Jeff was playing with these guys who weren't going to leave Toronto, and Tom swept in and took Jeff away from them. Tom was arrogant at the time; you learn humility later on. He had big ideas about what he wanted to do with the band, and he told you about it. But that led to a lot of bad feelings that never went away."

To move things along quicker, we started our own label in 1986, even as we worked on getting one of the big companies to sign us. We called it Forte — "loud and strong," in Italian. This was deliberate. People who spoke Spanish, French and Portuguese understood the meaning, while English-speakers could relate to discovering your "forte" — so we could communicate our message internationally.

"Jeff and Tom seemed to lead with most of the stuff, and Joe brought up the rear, so to speak," says Rich Chycki, the award-winning recording engineer who worked with us at Forte. "He's the one who really ran the studio, made sure it was maintained. If you wanted a gig with Healey, you'd probably have to go through Joe."

When people continued to question our management strategy, I had a ready line I'd pull out to shut them up: "So far, according to our accountant, we've done an okay job."

After our experience with B.B. King in Vancouver, things kept going our way. Another break came when the CBC invited Jeff to sit in with Stevie Ray Vaughan. If anyone in Canada hadn't heard about Jeff Healey, they would now. It was magic watching him and Stevie together, trading lick for lick — two greats playing off each other. I still get shivers thinking about it.

Like many groups starting out, we were sometimes over-reliant on cover tunes. Even today, a lot of fans remember Jeff for his unique renditions of "Like a Hurricane" and "All Along the Watchtower" and "While My Guitar Gently Weeps" — the latter with George Harrison, Jeff Lynne and Paul Shaffer. Where he still doesn't get his due is for his ability to write a great song. When I met him, he already had seven or eight in his arsenal. As we discussed the first song we should release on Forte, and threw out the names of different covers we'd done live, Jeff suddenly exploded.

"Fuck that," he said, his guitar in his lap, then launched into his original tune "Adrianna." With its beautiful melody, it blew our minds.

We also needed a B side, and used perhaps the most famous song Jeff ever wrote, "See the Light." As a rocking tune, "See the Light" was brilliant, and it deserved the acclaim it would receive. But let me assure you, "Adrianna," while never attracting the attention that it warranted, was in the same league.

As with other bar bands, we sold our record from the stage. What differentiated us from most groups was that everybody bought one.

Meanwhile, I was living in a little coach house, with another room that we used as the band's office. "I recall one evening in particular, where we started at the coach house. Tom just had to show me his new couch that he'd bought that day," Ben Richardson says. "It was nothing fancy, just a modest little two-seater covered in black fabric. But he was proud of it just the same. That night, we went out to see a band, ran into a couple of young ladies we knew and brought them back to the house to continue drinking. After a while, Tom disappeared upstairs with his lady friend, and I was able to enjoin my lady friend into giving me a blow job on the couch. Then we left.

Ben and Tom hanging out. I'm still pissed about my couch.

The next day Tom calls me up, livid. I guess I had left a stain on his brand-new couch that just would not come out. For some reason I was unable to feel any remorse."

We earned every excess. At that point, I was designing all the posters for the band. One night, Jeff came over to the coach house and demanded to assist.

"How are you going to help?" I said. "You can't see."

"I know how I want it done."

Jeff and I worked on these posters for hours. Then he slept on the notorious couch — banging his head on the ceiling beams whenever he'd stand up. The next morning, when he came downstairs, I told him, "Jeff, we can't use the posters."

"Are we still fighting over this shit?"

"No, the rats ate them."

Jeff didn't believe me. "Fuck off."

But I was telling the truth. My only explanation was that rats apparently liked the taste of Magic Marker. During the night, they'd shredded through the posters. They didn't eat anything else in the house.

As I've aged, I've grown to understand fear. Back then, I didn't. Nothing intimidated me. And that was a big benefit in the music business, since blues bands weren't supposed to get on the radio, let alone sell records. But we were too green to understand those principals.

Ignorance was bliss, and — for a certain time frame, at least — it served us well.

eight

If you watch our first video, "See the Light," you'd think we were *all* blind.

Without a major label behind us, no one was dressing or styling the band. Jeff's pants are practically up to his kneecaps. My headband and mustache make me look more like a dishwasher in a Lebanese restaurant than a rock 'n' roll drummer. Joe's wearing some bizarre combination of stripes — up, down and sideways.

Our strategy was getting the video out there, and grabbing the world's attention. That was the only way we figured that we were going to get signed. With a budget of $500 — which was a lot of money back then — we found a group of talented kids from the Ryerson School of Film in Toronto, who were just as hungry as we were to display their work to a wide audience. And — our fashion choices aside — "See the Light" was a pretty great showcase for the band. When Jeff jumps out of his chair and goes crazy on his guitar, it blows your fuckin' mind.

To this day, I'm indebted to the director, Alan Resnick, for conveying the excitement of the group. He understood exactly what we were about, and drew in people who might not have ever heard of us. Even without a record deal, we were soon getting regular airplay on MuchMusic, the Canadian version of MTV. That wasn't an easy thing to do, but we managed to break through. At the time, there were still people in high places in the music industry who got turned on when they heard a good song, and wanted to help the artist. It wasn't as corporate as it is now. Today, pulling off what we did would be pretty close to impossible.

Before you knew it, "See the Light" was getting played on the radio all over the place. People would run into us and want to hang out, be our friends, ride the wave right by our side. "Hey, Tom, what's cooking?" But once we had a taste of how big we could be, our eyes were set on America.

Sometimes I romanticize those days. No one was telling us what to do. The band was tight onstage and off. And when you see the way we're dressed, you know exactly what you're getting. We're representing nerds everywhere. If you want to look at the cool guys, go to your local gas station and watch them pump gas.

The tide was turning, and now it was our time.

• •

I'm not averse to taking advice from anybody. But when one of my childhood friends — a mailman named Zimmy — told me it would be a really cool thing if we played Dorchester Penitentiary, a maximum-security prison in New Brunswick, I wasn't particularly sold. Then he mentioned that he knew Jordi Morgan, a Maritimer who worked for MuchMusic and would probably want to cover the whole thing. Now that made sense. The publicity we'd get from being on MuchMusic would establish us as being far more than just another bar band. After discussing it with Jeff and Joe, we decided to give it a shot.

The folks at Dorchester, a 19th-century institution that conjured up images of hangings and beatings in dank cellars, had no interest in allowing cameras through the gates. But Jordi was excited now and kept asking around until he found another place down the road. Springhill, the childhood home of singer Anne Murray, had a modern, medium-security prison that looked more like a large elementary school — were it not for the razor-wire-topped fences.

Jeff was always quick to pick up on vibes, and as we walked into the building, he became quiet and withdrawn. Although Jeff didn't know that the hallways were dark, he could feel that we were in a scary place hidden away from the rest of society. He could hear the dull echoes of the inmates' voices in the distance, and the sound of doors creaking open and slamming shut. There was one checkpoint after another, where the guards checked our gear and our clothes and asked us questions in tones that suggested that they didn't think much more of us than they thought of the prisoners. Over and over, we were warned not to take anything from the inmates — letters to girlfriends, cigarettes, gum — and not to give them anything, either. If they asked for our phone numbers or addresses, we were told to say no. Otherwise we'd never get rid of these guys; each of us would be their lifeline outside of prison.

It was one of the few times, I think, that we all were nervous.

We were led into a large gymnasium and set up our gear while small groups of inmates lifted weights and played basketball. One by one, each prisoner grabbed a folding chair and wandered over to us. Our setup had the look of a school concert. There was no stage, and we were about seven feet from the front row.

"The guys from the weightlifting corner told us about the people they had beaten, robbed and killed in the past," says Jordi Morgan. "Then they told us how they'd never beaten, robbed or killed the people they were convicted of victimizing. We all quickly became pals. They asked if we could take letters to their girlfriends or moms. It was really an uncomfortable situation, but the music cut through everything."

One thing about our band: regardless of where we had to play, we were cocky enough to know we could pull it off. We had enough experience driving to gigs through snowstorms and playing outdoor shows in heat waves, sobering up when it was necessary to give the audience what they wanted. Yet in this circumstance, we felt like prisoners, too. We were locked into the building and surrounded by hostile guards, just literal feet from killers.

The lights were lowered. One, two, three — we kicked into "See the Light," to uproarious applause. Then, less a minute later, the circuit breaker failed and we descended into darkness. We heard the audience muttering and a few scattered boos. The tension was rising.

As always, Jeff could read the crowd. He also understood what had occurred without anyone telling him. As we stood, bathed in blackness, Jeff loudly asked the crowd, "What's the problem? Welcome to my world."

The blind reference worked; the place broke up. Now Jeff switched from music to comedy. He made the requisite joke about playing for a "captive audience," and added, "I hope I'm not keeping you guys from wherever you have to be later tonight." By the time that the lights came back on, the tension was gone. Everyone was having a good time. The whole vibe had changed, and as a result, the music was great.

As we came to the end, Jeff decided to introduce the band. Joe received a polite response. And, of course, Jeff got a big cheer. But I couldn't figure out why he decided to save me for last.

"And on the drums, we have . . ."

Then it all made sense.

"Hey, Tom! How's it going?!"

"What's up, Tom?! Haven't seen you in a while!"

Before I'd even realized it, Jeff had picked up on the fact that I knew a good chunk of the guys in the joint. It was funny at the time. But I also felt blessed for having dodged that bullet. I'd gotten involved with some bad people and been in the wrong place too many times. Fortunately, I was the guy who could step out into the bite of the cold winter air when the entertainment portion of the evening ended, not the one being brought back to his cell.

Jeff later mentioned the experience to me. He considered our visit to Springhill one of those special nights when he felt the people in the crowd, and understood some of the dark things they'd been through.

Somehow, it made the blues real.

• •

Because the people in my Lebanese support network had their hands in just about anything that could turn a buck, I'd known Tony Tobias for much of my life. He got involved in the music business managing his brother, singer-songwriter Ken Tobias, who wrote the million-selling soft rock classic "Stay Awhile" for the Bells, which hit number one in Canada and number seven in the U.S. in 1971. Tony had launched his own music publishing company, which represented Harry Belafonte's music catalog in Canada. A head television writer at the CBC, Tony worked with Gordon Lightfoot, Patsy Gallant and other artists, using music videos — then an untested concept — to promote them.

"Tom and I both grew up in Saint John, New Brunswick," Tony remembers. "He's younger than I am, maybe a generation younger. The Lebanese community in Saint John is tight, so the families knew each other. We use the term 'cousin' to describe ourselves, but use it loosely. Most certainly, we're not cousins, but that's how we think of ourselves.

"When everything started to come down with the Healey Band, they asked if I would work with them and put deals together internationally. My main concern was the publishing, because I'm a big believer in artists retaining their copyrights.

"I knew all of Tom's flaws. I knew all of his weak spots. And I would yell at him and tell him off and have fights with him because he could be belligerent and an asshole a hundred times over. And he made a lot of enemies that way because of the way he postured. But I also knew that in cases when I would have said no and walked away from a deal, he would hang in there and, almost every time, end up winning the deal.

"We all know Jeff Healey was a great guitar player. But in my view, if it wasn't for Tom — his hard-nosed business side, his dog-gedness, his acumen for breaking the rules — I seriously believe that Jeff would have only been a great local hero. And I don't care how much Stevie Ray Vaughan was excited about him, and everybody else coming through Toronto. I've seen this so many times over the years — "I could have been a contender" guys not prepared to leave their hometown. But I don't want to give too much credit to Tom. In terms of the success of the Jeff Healey Band — putting it together and making it work — it was all three of them."

After doing such an effective job of self-promotion, I expected an offer or two. I was even open to dealing with a Canadian label. But unfortunately, Jeff's reputation as a Toronto phenom meant that no one in his home city really saw him as an international star. Tired of waiting for the suitors to come to me, I put up my '77 Trans Am as collateral, borrowed a few thousand dollars from a friend and flew down to New York with our press kit and video on my lap. We knew that our fellow Canadian Paul Shaffer was working as the musical director for *Late Night with David Letterman* on NBC. Like every other musician from north of the border, Paul was a Jeff Healey fan. All I had to do was figure out a way to run into him, we thought, and he'd introduce me to all the right people.

We were naïve, but not completely stupid. I didn't anticipate an easy ride. This was the music "business" after all, and everybody was in it for his own selfish reason. While we wanted to become stars, the record companies wanted to make money as quickly as possible. Yes, some executives had long-term strategies, but most were only concerned about grabbing the next dollar. But what made it a great business — at least back then — was that, despite the greed, there was passion. It wasn't just lawyers and bean counters and drones looking for the next hit to keep their heads off the chopping block.

I knew all the stories about the sharks, the cokeheads, the scammers. But I'd watched my father get screwed by his partners — who then had the audacity to offer *me* a position. Believe me, I didn't have a lot of faith in human nature. I understood dysfunction and was ready to swim in this pool.

That was going to be a little challenging, since Shaffer had no idea I was coming. I walked around Rockefeller Center, trying to get backstage at the Letterman show, and nearly made it before security grabbed me. As they were escorting me out, though, fate intervened. No, I didn't find Shaffer. But Anton Fig, Letterman's drummer, spotted a logo on my T-shirt.

"Hey, Ayotte," he said, reading the name of the Vancouver-based custom drum company. "Are they any good?"

"Fuck yeah," I answered.

"Well, then, let's go talk about it."

Suddenly, he noticed that two security guards were holding me. But our connection as drummers was already established.

"Did you kill anybody?" he asked.

"No."

He motioned at security. "He's with me."

The two of us talked about music for a few minutes, then I pulled out our video and went looking for a VCR.

Anton had never seen Jeff perform and was pretty impressed by the video. "This guy's un-fuckin'-believable," he said. "Paul's gotta see this."

I could feel my blood pump a little bit faster. Was my plan about to actually come true? "Paul *Shaffer*? That's who I'm here to see."

But Shaffer wasn't around. So Anton told me about a record release party at the Bitter End, the Greenwich Village venue that had featured everyone from Woody Allen to Chuck Berry to Frank Zappa on its stage.

I didn't want to embarrass Anton by dropping his name at the door; I knew I might need him later, and couldn't afford any ill will. So I shook the doorman's hand and slipped him fifty bucks.

The guy looked down at the money. "Just don't give me any problems," he said.

Then I handed someone else another fifty dollars, and got a copy of the guest list. It turned out there were a number of record company executives at the event. I hung back for a while because I didn't want to overwhelm them like an amateur. But when the timing was right, I'd sidle up to my targets and make sure that no one left without a press kit and a video.

Mitchell Cohen, the A&R executive at Arista, remembers being handed one of our press kits by the label's head of rock promotion, Sean Coakley: "I was reading through the material and I saw that Albert Collins and other blues greats really liked Jeff. I'd just gotten into A&R and wanted to find a good rock act. So I booked a trip to Toronto to see the band. And it *was*, as everyone said, the kind of thing you had to see live. Jeff was charismatic and flamboyant with a masculine assertive voice that also showed some vulnerability. So when I got back to New York, I told my boss, Clive Davis, about the band."

Clive had signed just about every significant act to Arista: Aretha Franklin, the Grateful Dead, the Kinks. But lately, his proudest achievement was discovering singer Cissy Houston's daughter, Whitney, at a family concert and turning her into one of the best-selling artists of all time.

"I told Clive that every generation needs a Johnny Winter and a Carlos Santana," Cohen says, "and he understood. His idea was, 'This guy's a guitar hero. Let's find some great songs for him.' And that's how I brought the Arista people on board."

After I spoke to Mitchell, I immediately checked with Tony Tobias. Recalls Tony, "I get this phone call from Tom. And he says, 'Tony, do you know who a guy named Clive Davis is?' That shows you how much knowledge of the business he had. And I said, 'Yeah, he's the Beatles of record executives.'"

Had I truly understood what Clive meant to the industry, I might have acted unsure of myself when we finally met. Instead, I was convinced that once he heard our music — and sales pitch — he'd have no choice but to offer us a contract.

Looking back, I wholeheartedly believe that some labels discriminated against Jeff because of his disability. They saw a blind man onstage, and — regardless of how open-minded some of these executives claimed to be — felt so much discomfort that they wanted to turn away and pretend that he wasn't there. It really pissed me off. It *still* pisses me off. They wouldn't sign a guy who couldn't see, but they'd have no problem promoting a guy who couldn't *walk* because he was fucked up on heroin. If anyone was handicapped, it was these fuckin' executives — who were too blind themselves to appreciate the talent we were ready to hand deliver to them.

And then you had Clive Davis, who was comfortable not just pursuing Jeff but acknowledging his blindness. From the beginning, he told me, "I'm not interested in a circus act. I'm interested in one of the best talents I've ever heard play guitar."

Clive wanted Jeff to get down to New York as soon as possible and talk business. This was new territory for all of us, and I felt that we needed some coaching. So after I returned to Toronto, Tony Tobias arranged to meet Jeff and me at the Horseshoe Tavern.

For some reason, Joe didn't show up; maybe he had martial arts or something. But Jeff did, and Tony went to work.

"Jeff," he began, "I need to ask you something important. How much do you really want Tom and Joe to be part of this unit?"

"We're a team," Jeff answered. "It's the three of us. We're the Jeff Healey Band."

"The reason I'm asking you this is, when you get down there, you can bet there'll be guys who are going to try to carve the band up. 'I can find 30 bass players better than Joe. I can find one hundred drummers better than Tom.'"

"That doesn't mean anything to me."

"All right. So this is what's going to happen. When you meet Clive, he's going to be sitting behind a desk, and his desk is going to be raised. If he wants to talk music, then Jeff, you respond. But when it comes to talking business, Tom has to respond for you guys. Not everybody talking at the same time. That's the way it's got to be. You guys have to show solidarity so he knows you're committed to being there as a unit."

Tony turned his attention to me. "Something else," he said. "Clive's going to say, 'Okay, guys, I want to sign you.' Remember, Tom, he's got Whitney Houston, and Whitney's his baby. It's not the marketing department's baby. It's not the A&R department's. It's Clive's baby. And you want to be Clive's baby."

I wasn't sure where he was going. "What are you talking about, Tony?"

"Like I said, Clive's going to say he wants to sign you. I'm that sure of it. You don't meet an A&R guy at a club and get a meeting with Clive Davis if Arista's not very serious. And when he does, Tom, I want you to walk over to the desk, smash your fist onto it, lean into his face and say, 'If we sign with you, Clive, will you take personal responsibility for us?'"

Now, I understood. Clive was a gentleman, and Tony wanted us to have a gentleman's agreement. If we made it personal, it would no longer be a simple business arrangement. The moment Clive shook my hand, we'd get the kind of attention that he was devoting to Whitney. And then everyone else at Arista would know that if they wanted to ingratiate themselves with the king, it would serve them well to be extremely nice to us.

Interestingly, when I got back to New York with Jeff, he barely asked about our record deal. Back then, there were places to jam all over Manhattan, and Jeff wanted to play music. The night before the meeting, the two of us found a club and ended up getting hammered and hanging out until the shutters were coming down. And I have to say, we sounded pretty damn good.

Remarkably, we made it to our meeting on time. Clive was very gracious, and treated Jeff with the decorum he deserved. "What are your intentions?" he asked.

I could tell that Jeff was still a little trashed. "A few catchy songs for airplay, and a couple of all-out blues," he replied, conceptualizing our first album.

Clive nodded intently. Regardless of how much fun we'd had the night before, when the topic of music came up, Jeff always answered with conviction.

Now it was Clive's turn to talk. The man had seen a lot, and he wanted to tell us about it. But somewhere between Janis Joplin and Billy Joel, I could tell that Jeff had fallen asleep.

Fortunately, Clive didn't notice. He was a little bit in his own world at this point. And since Jeff had artificial eyes, he appeared to be wide awake, and taking in every gem.

Even under the best of circumstances, Clive can go on a little long; the man had lived a life. But we'd gone too far to turn into the trivia story about the goofy Canadian band that came all the way to New York only to blow it by snoring in Clive Davis's face.

Finally, Clive leaned across his desk and told us, very respectfully, "I'm going to sign you. If you want, I'd like to do a deal."

As Tony counseled, I asked Clive if he'd be willing to make us his personal responsibility. He seemed touched by the request.

Good thing I didn't bang on his desk.

"So I take it you're interested?" he said. Just as Tony predicted, Clive sounded a little paternal.

I sat back down and nudged Jeff hard enough to wake him. As if on cue, he smiled over at Clive and uttered, "Yes, Mr. Davis. Thank you very much."

CHAPTER
nine

Arista gave us a nine-album deal, an indication that Clive was starting to see Jeff as his new "baby." With the help of a very tough lawyer named Richard Hahn, we worked out a deal to keep Canada to ourselves. They'd distribute our albums there, but we'd own the rights and release the songs on our separate label. From what my research told me, no Canadian band had ever gotten a better agreement from an American label.

Although we knew very little about promotion — at least the way it was done at Arista's level — we were defensive about the way Jeff's disability would be marketed. "We don't want to see anything with the word 'blind' on it," Joe insisted to *Canadian Musician* magazine. "That's irrelevant."

It felt like we were the masters of our destiny, but I remembered a time when my father felt the same way — before he lost everything. I also never forgot how he urged me to take my drums along to Toronto. Now it was time to balance everything out. With the money I was making in the Healey Band, I hired a lawyer to sue the bank that had helped put my dad out of business. It took a while, but we beat them. He won and was able to live comfortably on the proceeds of that lawsuit for the rest of his life.

Arista sent us on a tour around select cities of the United States to showcase the band. At one stop, we were scheduled to open for and back up Chuck Berry, who was notoriously cheap and didn't like paying for his own musicians or gear. "I count to four before every song," he growled at us before we went on. "I start the song. You follow me. Don't fuck up."

We played a few songs before he kicked over to "Johnny B. Goode." Jeff being Jeff, he decided to start ripping into leads while giving me time to find the pocket. Chuck was cursing at me and cursing at Joe and then, when he looked back at Jeff, something clicked. Suddenly, Jeff and Berry were jamming. Joe and I were in awe, watching our bandmate trade licks with the godfather of guitar-driven rock 'n' roll.

When the show ended, Chuck walked over to Jeff and seemed to grudgingly shake his hand. All he would say was, "You're a muthafucka."

That was the tour when we played live on MTV. For any young band during that era, that was your ticket to stardom. But we were still buzzing about Chuck Berry.

Our first album, *See the Light*, was a combination of songs Jeff had written and tracks that Clive went out and found for us. In retrospect, that became a problem because Jeff really was a good songwriter — Joe and I weren't — and could have carried more of that load. But Clive wasn't very considerate of that side of him, and at that early stage, it bruised Jeff and, I think, long term, forced an overreliance on other peoples' songs. But when I listen to *See the Light* and hear one of Jeff's original compositions, like "I Need to

Be Loved," my reaction is the same as it was the first time I heard it. It's a strong song, and Jeff should have been encouraged to do more.

"I write about things that everyday people understand," Jeff said in an interview with *Musician* magazine's Ted Drozdowski. "I won't write about politics, which a lot of people can take or leave. But love between human beings is a natural thing, so we can all relate to it. And if I get to play some guitar in the bargain, then everybody's happy."

In total, Jeff is credited on almost half the songs on the album: "I Need to Be Loved," "My Little Girl," "Don't Let Your Chance Go By," "That's What They Say," and the title track, "See the Light." All three of us and British guitarist Robbie Blunt are listed as the cowriters of "Nice Problem to Have." To be honest, I didn't feel I deserved a mention at all. The song was a free-flowing jam, and if you listen, there are no drums on the track. It's really a traditional blues piece with bass and guitar riffs. Originally, we had no intention of including this on the album. But when we listened to the recording, we loved it. So we were sitting around, talking about what to name the song, and couldn't come up with anything. And suddenly, it hit me. We were in L.A., having a good time, and the biggest challenge in our lives seemed to be what to call a song that Arista planned to release internationally.

"It's a nice problem to have," I told Jeff.

And it was. A few months ago, I was wandering around Rockefeller Center, hoping to run into Paul Shaffer. Now we had an unprecedented publishing deal, with sublicensing deals in every territory. The Jeff Healey Band had bet on itself and won.

Arista wasn't going to spare anything for our debut. We were sent to L.A. to record, put up at an apartment complex called the Oakwood, and assigned two superstars, Thom Panunzio and Greg Ladanyi, to coproduce the album. As I mentioned earlier, Thom — the future executive senior vice president of Universal Music Group — had been in the studio with every important rock star of the previous decade; if you watch the Springsteen documentary *The Promise: The Making of Darkness on the Edge of Town*, you'll see a lot of Panunzio. Our time with him was going to be limited, though, because he had a prior commitment to work with U2 on *Rattle and Hum*.

Ladanyi's credits included Fleetwood Mac, Don Henley, Jackson Browne and the Jackson family. He was everything I imagined a big shot in the record business to be: a fast-living ladies' man. Greg loved rock 'n' roll so much that he literally died on the job; while touring Cyprus with Greek singer Anna Vissi in 2009, he slipped and fell 13 feet off a ramp leading to the stage and fractured his skull. During sessions, he had a reputation as a taskmaster — or a "dictator," in Panunzio's words — and managed to piss me off pretty quickly.

"The two of us were in a room together, on a conference call with Tom," Panunzio recalls. "Greg knew Tom only as the manager of the Healey band, and starts talking about the drums. Greg was a perfectionist with drums. And he's saying, 'I know you want what's best for the band, and some kid from Canada, or whoever you have, ain't gonna cut it in this world. This is big-time, and we need to bring in one of the top studio drummers.' I'm jumping up and down and waving my hands around, but Greg doesn't notice. And then Tom says, very sternly, 'Greg, you're talking to the drummer.' Greg just goes, 'I didn't know that. Okay.' And that was the end of the conversation."

There was another reason why we weren't 100 percent sold on him. Ladanyi was a mainstream pop guy, and we were all worried that the record would sound a little too slick. The first couple of rough mixes didn't impress us, and Jeff expressed it — far more diplomatically than he would later on, when his status rose. Given Greg's background, I thought he might push back and say, "Hey, this is the way we do things here." Instead, he seemed to genuinely want to capture the spontaneous mood we had at our shows.

"I haven't done this kind of thing before," he told Jeff, almost apologetically.

Once he understood what we wanted, we were in synch. Greg helped Jeff experiment with different sounds and gave us a sense of arrangement. Still, many of the drum, rhythm guitar and bass parts you hear on *See the Light* were recorded live off the floor. Interestingly, it was Jeff who insisted that the LP be more than a guitar album.

"There are actual songs with verses, choruses and bridges," he told *Canadian Musician* after the album was released in 1988. "It's very dependent on the vocals and lyrics. I didn't want to make an album just for guitar players."

In the same article, Joe emphasized that this was a rock and not a blues record: "A blues album tends to be more musician-oriented, but a good rock album is more focused on songs."

Things were going really well. Panunzio and I instantly related to each other, both personally and professionally. He was an extremely perceptive guy. Yet — like me, at the beginning — he had a hard time grasping that Jeff was blind.

"We were in a real big room with padded walls, almost like an insane asylum," he remembers. "The room was so big that Greg Ladanyi would hit golf balls around on breaks. But I'd notice that Jeff would walk around that room all the time without help. He'd put down his guitar and go out to the lounge to use the bathroom or get a cup of coffee, and he'd go right to the door and open it like someone who had perfect vision. I also noticed that he was snapping his fingers all the time, but I just thought that he was grooving, you know? Music going through his head. But then he explained that, because the room was padded and the door was wood, the sound of the door would reflect back to him when he snapped his fingers. So that's how he figured it out."

Stevie Salas, a guitarist, producer and TV host who's played with Rod Stewart, Aerosmith, Terence Trent D'Arby, Justin Timberlake and so many others — and was the music director on Mick Jagger's solo work, as well as *American Idol* — was driving down Sunset Boulevard once and saw Jeff by himself, just kind of wandering around in the parking lot of the Rainbow, a place that's still pretty popular with musicians. "He didn't have his crew with him," Stevie says. "He was just by himself. And, you know, he's blind. So I stop the car and roll down the window. And I scream, all the way from Sunset Strip, in the middle of this giant crowd, with all this noise, 'Hey, Jeff!' And he just stops and goes, 'Stevie!' He recognized my voice right away."

It was Clive who persuaded us to record the song that became our first big hit, "Angel Eyes," and I admit that I wasn't happy with the suggestion. He first played me a recording of the song — written by music industry vets John Hiatt and Fred Koller — in his office and, believe me, it didn't sound anything like the version our fans would come to know. It sounded like crap. But Clive was really stuck on it.

"I know a few things about hits, Tom, and this can be a hit."

Once we got to L.A., I knew we'd have to take a crack at "Angel Eyes." But I couldn't shake my apprehension. Every time I expressed these misgivings to industry veterans, they told me, "Hey, if Clive likes it so much, there has to be a reason. Work at it."

We tortured ourselves with that song. None of us were feeling it. But I kept telling myself that Clive Davis couldn't be wrong about it. And then, one night in the studio, it all came together. After messing with an acoustic version, Jeff grabbed his electric and began decoding the greatness in the song.

It was probably about 2 a.m. Jeff started nodding off, then suddenly he woke up and had this melody. It didn't sound anything like the song Clive played me in his office. This was Jeff Healey's "Angel Eyes," a rendition heavily influenced by the country tunes he liked as a kid. And it worked. As soon as Jeff got into it, Joe and I were on board. "Fuck the original," we said. "This is how we're going to do it." All three of us knew we had a smash hit.

Hiatt also wrote "Confidence Man," a blues everyman's song, for *See the Light*. John's one of the most respected guys in the business, and I know why Clive funneled his songs to us. Clive doesn't do anything unless he thinks it's going to go platinum. The downside, though, is that those commercial considerations run counter to the rough-and-ready band that we were. During our time with Arista, we'd end up laying down a number of radio-friendly tracks that were a lot more white-bread than what we imagined going in.

Back then, Jeff saw his competition as people like Stevie Ray Vaughan and Robert Cray — and ended up being more in the Robert Cray arena than the Stevie Ray arena. Which isn't bad, by the way. Robert Cray has five Grammys on his shelf. But we still considered ourselves more in the Stevie Ray tradition of balls to the walls, hit 'em hard blues-rock.

As a rule, we were pretty happy with the first album. The songs feel emotional and spontaneous. You can hear a certain freedom in the way the solos are improvised. Jeff told a reporter that he approached *See the Light* like a jazz musician, switching from one style to another: "We weren't showcasing . . . it's just what we do. The worst thing you can do is separate out a style which you want to go with. You shut down your range of creativity."

When we got tired of the studio, we'd drive around Los Angeles, looking for a place to jam, bringing along our buddy Chuck Reed to work the soundboard and as a guitar tech. He was maybe 17 or 18 — I think he barely had his license — smoked his weed like a California surfer kid, and fell in love with the band.

We didn't know L.A. that well, so Chuck invited us out to his family's house in Malibu. It was an exquisite place and, as I looked around, I spotted these plaques all over the wall. It turned out that Chuck's grandfather was Alan Reed, the voice of Fred Flintstone — Chuck also had an uncle who was Fred Astaire's choreographer, Hermes Pan — but you'd never know it from talking to him. He was just so understated and worked really hard to impress us as a good roadie.

Chuck noticed that we were accumulating a lot of equipment. Jeff had gone out in L.A. one day and tried out a bunch of guitars — Rickenbacker, Ibanez — before stumbling on an instrument he'd never seen before: a black Jackson 6- and 12-string doubleneck. As he remembered, "It had everything on it that I wanted. I could play both necks at the same time. I had four hands . . . It's perfect." That joined his black Fender Squier Strat and white standard Strat as an essential part of his gear. Chuck wanted to make sure we could fit all our equipment in his vehicle. So he pulled out a saw and — as we stood there in amazement — altered the car specifically for us.

"I cut out everything behind the driver's seat and put up a big roof to make it look like a house," he says. "We'd put all the gear in there. And when we'd pull up in front of the gig, everyone would stop and look. Then they'd go inside, see Jeff jump off the stage and start running around the audience — with his guitar still on his knees. If you weren't a fan before, you instantly became one. It was awesome."

Jeff wasn't particular about where he played. One day, we were walking by the Beverly Center and talked the pizza joint guy into letting us jam there. We brought all our gear into the mall on a Friday night, set up and just started going. And it was great. A couple of kids really liked us and invited us to a party after the pizza joint closed — like we were a bunch of teenagers again. We drove around Beverly Hills, got to the gate, gave the proper name to security and were waved in. Then we started down the road toward a pretty nice house. But it wasn't the main house. It was the freakin' maid's quarters.

Finally we found where we needed to go. I remember sitting in the living room, looking around and asking myself, "What does this kid's father do for a living?" I mean, one minute we're jamming in a pizza joint, then we're in this mansion in Beverly Hills. Not exactly what we're used to.

No one in Canada was taking us back to their mansions.

Still, there were aspects of this new life that none of us liked. Jeff hated being told what to do — that's why he couldn't even finish high school — and now the label wanted him to work with a stylist.

"You're the star of the band. You need the proper look."

Here's Jeff exact response: "I'm a blue-collar guy."

He didn't mind being a little chubby; to him, food was a delightful vice. Hamburgers, fries, soda by the gallon. At one point, he switched to diet soda, but he still kept his baby fat. People don't understand that it isn't the sugar that doubles your gut, it's the carbonation.

He didn't give a flying fuck if his shoes were pointy or his pants were straight. But overnight, there were people around telling Jeff how to cut his hair and pestering him to work out. He hated it — hated the bullshit he had to deal with, when all he wanted to do was play music — but he went along with the suggestions. In fact, Joe stepped forward and volunteered to become Jeff's workout partner — a situation that continued when we got back to Canada and they both moved into the same building at 53 McCaul Street. Joe knew Jeff couldn't stand working out, but would knock on his door and get him to exercise.

Now, here's the interesting thing. As much as Jeff resented being placed on a regimen, when we went out he enjoyed the attention he got. He'd always been handsome, and now, when we hit the town, people would see him in his new threads and stop in their tracks. *Who's that guy?* That's the kind of impression he made. And this is in Hollywood, where looks mean everything. This was the place to be on top of your game, and we weren't losing, we were winning.

Sometimes, though, I think I enjoyed this period a lot more than Jeff did. And I really believe that's because Jeff wasn't able to see. He just didn't understand the whole image thing. I believe that every great blind entertainer has been surrounded by stylists: José Feliciano with his dark shades, Stevie Wonder with his dreads, Andrea Bocelli in his fashionable tux. All these guys had people who staged their look to match their artistry. And just as with Jeff, the strategy worked.

Of course, when you're the sensation that's blown into town, the sharks find you pretty fast — the managers who want to take the band over, the musicians who think they're better than those goofs standing behind the lead singer. It was everything Tony Tobias had warned him about, and Jeff was loyal. He could have had *the* best guys, and he stuck with us.

It was the three of us. The Jeff Healey Band. We were a team, and no one was going to get in the way.

At least for the time being.

CHAPTER

ten

One of Jeff's favorite activities when we were relaxing on the tour bus
was watching movies on video. He was an astute listener and followed the plots closely. While the rest of us would get distracted by
things we saw — either on the bus or out the window — Jeff kept his
focus. I can't remember a single time when he asked, "What's going
on here?"

Nonetheless, I don't think any of us ever imagined that Jeff would
end up on the big screen himself. But while we were solidifying our
reputation, a writer named David Lee Henry was watching us play in
Toronto. Later, he and a future Oscar-winning screenwriter named
Hilary Henkin came up with a movie script that included a blind
singer with a taste for the blues. The script found its way to Joel
Silver, who'd recently been producing action classics like *48 Hrs.*,

Predator and the soon-to-be-released *Die Hard*. At the time, he was the biggest producer in Hollywood. And naturally, he knew Clive.

Clive told Joel he had the perfect candidate for the role of Cody, the blind singer in the film that became *Road House*.

I wasn't too crazy about the idea of cross-promoting our music with a major motion picture. Jeff was already pissed off about having to listen to a stylist. We didn't need another legion of suits to take us further away from our music. But, really, we had no choice. As Clive explained, the script called for a rock 'n' roll trio fronted by a blind guy. Well, there was only one rock 'n' roll trio fronted by a blind guy, and that was us.

"Go out and meet Joel Silver," Clive told me. "Don't tell Jeff just yet. Just go there, have your meeting and see what you think."

So here I was, having yet another L.A. experience for the first time: standing outside the cave of the dragon at a movie studio, waiting for my audience with Joel Silver. People were screaming. Assistants were running in and out. One woman flew by me in tears. "Holy fuck," I said to myself. "It's really like this?"

Finally, Silver called me in. I could see that he had a thousand things going on and wasn't sure if I was there for a meeting or to deliver the Chinese food.

"Who are you?"

I paused. "I'm the guy in the band you're thinking of putting in your movie. Clive Davis . . ."

"Oh, yeah, yeah, yeah. Your guy . . ."

He was talking about Jeff.

". . . what kind of guy is he? Has he got any brains?"

"He's brilliant."

"Well, what does he look like? I've never seen him."

Naturally, I had a copy of the video I'd used to shop for a label. Joel let out a shout, and suddenly, someone was in his office, slipping the video into the VCR. Silver leaned forward and listened. I could see him twist his head slightly, studying Jeff. He didn't have to tell me anything for me to know that he was impressed.

"Can this kid act?"

How the fuck was I supposed to know? But I'd seen Jeff turn on the charm to some pretty obnoxious people, so my instinct told me he could. "He's a natural." I tried to imagine Jeff memorizing lines. "He's a fuckin' blind guy who never forgets a voice. You meet him once, and run into him six years later, and he goes, 'Hey, Joel, what's going on?'" Now I was feeling confident. "So now you're asking me if he won't be able to remember some line in a movie?"

Clearly, I was saying the things Joel wanted to hear — in the brash tone to which he was accustomed. "Well, I'd like to meet this guy Jeff Healey. And if I like him, we'll put you in the movie. All three of you." He held up a finger, as if to warn me. "But I want to let you know, the band's just for background . . ."

"I understand that," I interrupted. "But once you meet Jeff, once you see him play live, you might decide to do a little more with him."

Joel leaned back on his chair and smirked. "Are you running Hollywood now?"

When I told Jeff about the latest development in the fast-moving career of the Jeff Healey Band, he showed minimal enthusiasm. "Why am I meeting some movie guy?" he asked.

I explained the marketing strategy. We already had an album coming out. If we were in a movie, too, it would mean tens of thousands of new fans. So I returned to Joel's office with Jeff. The difference was that, as Jeff walked around the building, he couldn't see the posters and the awards and the way people looked at Joel Silver with a mixture of veneration and terror. So when Joel said, "I'm trying to decide whether I want you to be in the movie or not," Jeff coolly replied, "I'm trying to decide the same thing."

Joel was totally impressed. Shooting was supposed to start immediately. United Artists needed its own soundtrack, of course. Which meant that in addition to recording *See the Light*, we were now recording the music for *Road House*.

We'd been in the studio from the moment we'd landed at LAX. It was an exhausting grind; when Clive told us we'd be working 28 out of 24 hours, he wasn't exaggerating. But the soundtrack was being supervised by Jimmy Iovine, a brilliant, brassy Brooklyn guy — the son of a longshoreman — who was just on the cusp of becoming a legend in the business. In 1990, Jimmy would found Interscope and, two years later, sign Tupac Shakur as the first of the label's many hip hop acts. While we were working on *Road House*, he assured me, "Rap is going to be the future."

I was too thick to realize that I was talking to a visionary. "Jimmy, who the hell cares about rap? Rap is what you do when you're in college and everyone's supposed to be studying for exams. You smoke a couple of joints, stay up all night and rap, rap, rap — telling stupid stories to your friends because you don't want to study. Then you wake up in the morning, go to class and flunk. Who the hell cares about rap?"

Wow. The things you'd like to take back.

Jeff had been sitting next to me. He was no rap fan, either. But he appreciated the beats and realized that it was a viable form of music. Two or three years later, we'd hear a hip hop record on the radio, and Jeff would nudge me and say, "Flunk any exams lately?"

But it's not as if Jeff was always right. I was with Jeff and Joe when we first heard Lenny Kravitz's "Let Love Rule." It blew my mind. "This guy's going to be huge," I predicted.

Jeff and Joe laughed at me. "This is the worst crap I ever heard," Jeff said. "He's not going anywhere."

A few short years later, Jeff was honored when Lenny joined us onstage in both Europe and North America. Jeff and Lenny were both guys who could play any instrument, and they loved hanging out after a concert and jamming at some out-of-the-way joint. I remember watching the two of them in a bar one night from the audience, in amazement like everyone else. When the jam ended, I reminded Jeff about his comment about Lenny. "This guy Lenny Kravitz," I smirked. "He's not going anywhere. Right?"

After biting his lip and curling his hair, Jeff realized that I was getting him back for his "flunk any exams" remarks. Jeff was a *gotcha* kind of guy and I very seldom got him. He was too quick.

Jeff and me with Lenny Kravitz after the jam.

Looking back, I can't believe I was so disrespectful to Jimmy Iovine when he shared his insights about hip hop, and I'm shocked he tolerated me afterwards. Fortunately, he seemed to like me. I know that he definitely liked the band. In the studio, he'd get a sound check then let us go to work. Everything was recorded live. Then he'd select our best stuff for *Road House*. One of our leftovers, our interpretation of ZZ Top's "Blue Jean Blues," wound up on *See the Light*.

A number of the music icons wanted to come by and see Jeff. When we recorded the Doors song "Roadhouse Blues" for the movie, there wasn't a person in the studio who didn't love it. Then Jimmy Iovine realized that no one had bothered to ask for permission from the Doors keyboardist, Ray Manzarek, who controlled the band's catalog. Ray could be a difficult guy, Jimmy said, and everybody was a little bit on edge. But Ray said he'd come over to the studio and listen to what we did.

The executives who were involved in this process wanted to make Ray happy, so they ordered a bunch of sushi. We didn't even eat sushi, but nobody asked us. Jeff hated the smell of fish and could barely stay in the room. Manzarek came in, put a few pieces of sushi on a plate and listened to the recording.

When the song ended, Manzarek maintained an impassive expression. Then he clapped once, paused, clapped twice and smiled.

That was how Ray gave us permission to use "Roadhouse Blues." He hung around for a while and was very friendly, talking musician talk. But that's because he liked the song. The sushi had nothing to do with it.

A few months later, I was going through some bills and noticed an unusually large expense. It was the bill for the sushi — for hundreds of dollars. You know who those millionaires charged for the food we didn't even want to eat? *Us.*

The *Road House* plot revolves around James Dalton, a bouncer with a mysterious past. Patrick Swayze was the perfect actor for the lead role. But he and I got off to a very bad start. Jeff and I were hanging out in the studio one afternoon when Patrick stormed in and started berating us.

"Who are you fuckin' guys and why are you doing this music? Nobody okayed this with me." I was sitting behind the drums and didn't even look at Swayze's face. I just heard some asshole yelling at us, and decided to do something about it.

"I don't know what your problem is."

"My problem?" he asked in disbelief. "No, I think you have the problem. You really fucked up just now." And then he stormed out the door.

Before the band could start joking about the blowhard who'd had the nerve to barge in on us, the engineer pointed out, "You know who that is, right? That's Patrick Swayze."

Fuck! I ran out of the room, followed Swayze down the stairs and came up behind him in the parking lot. And then I noticed that he was driving what I thought was a silver Bricklin. Not a lot of people knew about the Bricklin, a gull-wing-door sports car, but I did because it was assembled in Saint John, New Brunswick. I should have been apologizing, but I couldn't help myself from saying, "Hey, Patrick? Is that a Bricklin? Is that car a piece of shit or what? That Lucas Electrical System sucks."

He was still in an ornery mood. "What the fuck do you know about it?"

"I know a lot about it. I'm from New Brunswick. I've walked through the factory, man. I've been on the assembly line."

Patrick's mood suddenly changed. "No way." He smiled. "I guess it is kind of a piece of shit." He surveyed the car, then looked over at me. For the next few minutes, we talked about the car. Then Patrick asked, "What the fuck are you guys doing here, anyway?"

"That blind guy you were yelling at — the one I was defending — that's one of the best guitar players in the world — maybe the best, actually — and he's one of my closest friends. Almost like a brother. I can't let anyone come in the room and start giving him shit. I'm sure you understand that. And there's no need to yell at him, anyway. He's just down here doing his gig, man. We just got signed to our first album, and now they asked us to do the soundtrack to the movie. No one wanted to offend you or anything . . ."

"Look, man, I'm sorry," he responded. "It's just that all these decisions get made that nobody tells me about."

We talked a little bit more, and he mentioned that he fancied himself a guitar player. So I brought him into the studio and introduced him to everyone, and we all started playing. He was an acoustic hacker with a good voice. He held his own. Over the next few weeks, we hung out quite a bit — so much so that Patrick and Jeff even talked about doing a duet together. Clive and Joel never were able to come to terms on that. But I think Patrick could have pulled it off.

It was Patrick who educated us on how weird it was to be a star. Not long after we met, the two of us were in a bar and noticed two chicks checking him out. "You want to see something," he smirked, taking a drag on his cigarette. "Watch this."

He crushed out his butt and stood it up by the filter on the table.

And you know what happened? Those girls began fighting over it. Not arguing, but pushing and shoving each other.

"Now you see what my life is like," he explained.

It all made sense. When people fight over your cigarette butt, it warps you. You feel entitled to barge into a studio and start screaming at strangers. It's great to have star power, but this was fuckin' crazy.

Soon Patrick became our good friend. He was fascinated by Jeff, particularly the way women were drawn to him. "Don't take this the wrong way," Patrick asked Jeff on the set, "but how does a blind guy make a move on a girl?"

A few seconds later, a stunning actress passed by, and Jeff showed him.

"Excuse me," he began. "You know I can't see you, but it's just that . . . you *sound* so beautiful."

Patrick folded his arms, watching as Jeff went on about his ability to "hear" beauty — and he knew this actress had it. "Wow," she responded, "that's really nice."

Jeff reached out, claiming that he could braille her good looks with his fingertips. But he was extremely polite about it. "Do you mind if I touch?"

"Of course, Jeff. I would love that."

Suddenly, Jeff lowered his hands and honked the woman's breasts. A photographer on the set caught a picture of Jeff, Patrick and the actress all rolling with laughter.

Nowadays, we would have been thrown out of Hollywood, and I wouldn't be writing this book.

As Jeff said in an interview with *Music Scene* magazine, "For somebody who got into this business to have fun, there sure are a lot more people taking things a lot more seriously than I do."

Because most of *Road House* takes place in a bar, we were surrounded by vats of fake beer all day — until Jeff and I decided to slip one of the prop guys fifty bucks to bring us real beer instead. No one seemed to enjoy this more than Patrick. One day, he and Jeff were

outside, sitting on a fence, hammered, telling jokes. At one point,
Patrick said, "Man, Jeff, you are so fuckin' funny," and smacked him
in the chest. Jeff lost his balance and didn't know where to fall. So
he went feet-backwards, and Patrick leaned over to catch him. The
two of them rolled down a hill, landed safely and just continued what
they'd been doing, talking and laughing.

Former professional wrestling champion Terry Funk always
seemed to be nearby during these incidents. Terry was a fun-loving,
crazy Texan who knew how to make the barroom brawl scenes in

Having a laugh with Sam Elliot on the Road House *set.*

Road House look believable. He could also party harder than all of us combined, but his wife kept a pretty tight leash on him. I found it hysterical when his wife would call the set, trying to monitor Terry's whereabouts, and this big tough wrestler would beg Jeff to answer the phone. "Just tell Mama I'll be home a little late," he'd plead.

As exciting as it was to make a movie, it was also incredibly boring. You'd get there at six in the morning and sit around playing cards until someone said it was time for your shot. By lunchtime, we'd be crawling up the walls. So since we had our instruments on the set, we'd start jamming. Sometimes Patrick would play with us. Grips would show up, cameramen, audio techs — all these cool, creative guys who enjoyed attending a 15-minute jam session in the middle of the workday. After a while, Patrick and the other star of

Road House, Sam Elliott, began inviting friends who were working on other soundstages. So by the time our first album came out, we had a nice little buzz going in L.A.

Patrick told everyone — from fellow actors to journalists — that Jeff helped humanize Swayze's character in the movie. And he made himself available to us when we weren't sure how to do business the Hollywood way. I'd been noticing that the longer the project went on, the more Jeff's scenes increased. They were rewriting the script, giving him more lines. Jeff said he found acting in *Road House* easy because "I was playing a character modeled very closely after myself. I'd done some acting . . . since I was eight. It was a matter of putting it all together and be as natural as possible."

Everyone agreed that Jeff was doing a great job in front of the camera. Still, we hadn't worked out our movie deal yet. I had no idea what we were supposed to get paid. When I told Patrick about our dilemma, he told us we were in a very good place.

"Don't worry about anything," he said. "Let's just keep shooting. Let them put you in every fuckin' scene. The more they shoot the movie, they can't get rid of you. You've got them by the balls."

I took the advice and waited a few weeks until I approached Joel about our situation. "I don't understand what's going on," I told him. "We're working our ass off for you, and we have no paper. We have a record deal, but no movie deal. You guys are paying our costs and all that, but what's going on with our money?"

Joel started doing his Hollywood routine, warning me that I shouldn't be asking questions to a guy of his stature in that kind of tone. And then he actually told me, "You pull that shit, you'll never work in this town again." He really said it — although I was never sure if he was joking.

The timing couldn't have been better. We'd committed to a gig in Vancouver that we'd told Joel about weeks before. So every day, I was reminding Rowdy Herrington, the director, "Look, we need to get up to Canada on Thursday. Probably won't be back until Monday. But shit, if we don't have a deal, I don't know if we're coming back at all."

Just before we were supposed to leave, I got an angry call from Joel: "You guys aren't going anywhere."

"Joel, we are going somewhere. I've been telling you about this for weeks, and nothing's happened. We've been making this movie, and technically we don't even work for you. We don't have a contract, so we're under no obligation to stay."

He blustered a little more, but I knew we had the edge at this point. I called the roadies and was watching them pack our equipment into two vans when Joel made a personal appearance.

"Where are you guys going?"

"To the airport. Where do you think we're going?"

It goes without saying that I had no intention of staying in Vancouver and blowing off our movie deal. But once we got to Canada, I threw myself into the process of just *playing* again. No suits. No politics. No bullshit. When we arrived back in L.A., Patrick was waiting with a big smile. "Joel's been worried you guys weren't coming back." He threw an arm around Jeff. "What a ballsy move."

"What's so ballsy about it?" Jeff answered. "No one's paid us. I'm a musician. I play, I get paid. I'm not here for this movie star shit."

There were plenty of observers around, and the conversation was repeated verbatim to Joel Silver. The next time we spoke, his lawyer ordered us off the set. "Don't even bother coming back," he announced.

"Okay," I said. "But I have a question. What's going to happen to all that dialogue between Patrick and Jeff? Are you going to reshoot those scenes with another musician, or just throw everything in the garbage? I mean, you've probably shot three-quarters of the movie by now."

The lawyer promised to get back to me.

It was a good move for everyone involved. Anybody who's seen *Road House* remembers Jeff as much as Swayze. Jeff's Toronto accent could have posed a problem — the bar in the movie is supposed to be in Jasper, Missouri — but the studio took care of that by hiring a voice coach. Because of what had happened with the stylist, I expected Jeff to resist. But Jeff really liked the girl who became his voice coach. In addition to working on the twang, he needed to play his character convincingly — his most memorable line involved him grabbing Patrick and saying, "I thought you'd be bigger" — and he and the coach spent hours talking. That's what Jeff really found attractive — a woman who could reach him on that level. I know that his voice coach occupied his thoughts quite a bit; he developed a major crush on her.

But none of us were one-woman men during our time in L.A. Jeff and I had been introduced to a pair of beauty queens at some point and were hanging out with them regularly.

Once again, Patrick ended up teaching us a lesson about the currency of Hollywood. He explained that we were now associating with movie stars. Not as flunkies or gophers, but as equals. That meant that a new quality of woman found the members of the Jeff Healey Band desirable.

As our song said, this was yet another good problem to have. The party was just getting started, and none of us were about to stop to ponder whether this kind of excess would inevitably have consequences.

CHAPTER
eleven

That sushi bill was a wakeup call. We were a commodity, an ATM machine.
During the day, we shot *Road House*. Then, when everyone else went
home or went out at the end of the workday, we locked ourselves in
the studio and recorded the album. As long as the product reached
the shelves, no one gave a fuck about us. We were no different than
those kids weaving designer sweaters in some sweatshop in Indonesia.

Jeff was the first one to realize what was going on. I'm not going
to say it was because he was blind, but in some ways it was. While
other people's eyes were wide open, taking in all the visual stimulation, Jeff was *listening* and processing what the rest of us couldn't.

You could argue that all three of us were blind when it came to
show business. But, as they say, ignorance is bliss.

Joe was oblivious. He wanted to be a star and it was happening.

And I wasn't much better. I was so caught up in the business of the Jeff Healey Band — making deals, making contacts — that I didn't understand why Jeff was bitching.

Then again, as much as he'd never admit it, Jeff was getting sucked into the culture of Hollywood. Even at that early stage. He was the star of our group and was learning that he needed to keep himself the center of attention. So he'd gossip, stir shit up, play Joe and I against each other, keep us off-balance. If he was talking to a record company guy, he'd say things, like, "Tom never told *me* that. I don't know what he's talking about." And the record company guy would start bashing me because it was so important to him to make the star happy.

Meanwhile, people were getting in my ear, too. Jimmy Iovine and I were getting along great and started forming a relationship separate from the rest of the band. So he made me an offer: he and I would manage the band as partners and find a drummer to replace me. He was going to start a label and wanted me to move on with him to other ventures.

Here's how he said it: "Look, you're a great manager. You're an okay drummer. Drummers are a dime a dozen. There's a million good drummers, but there aren't a lot of good managers. There's a lot we can do together."

I truly believe that Jimmy was sincere. He didn't want me to do anything to screw Jeff and Joe. In fact, my replacement would probably have been a better drummer than me. But I couldn't break the symmetry of the group. We were a band. We'd pledged fidelity to each other when we were jamming at Grossman's. Now, before our first album even hit the stores, I wasn't going to leave my friends because something better or more interesting came along.

"Tom didn't even think twice about his decision," says Chuck Reed, who'd later work very closely with Jimmy Iovine. "He was with Jeff and that was the end of it. And, regardless of what you think about what happened later, he ended up spending the next couple of years in an awesome band."

Would Jimmy have been good for the group? Definitely. A little guy like me has to scrap all day for the things someone like Jimmy can solve with one phone call. But what happens when things go bad? I knew I'd keep fighting for the band, no matter what. I wasn't sure that anyone else would be willing to do that.

So I just flat out told Jimmy no. I can't say I regretted the decision. But I did question it years later, when the band fell apart and everybody was slamming Tom Stephen for fucking everything up.

I will say this. At this stage, Jeff was just as loyal to me as I was to him. Almost every day, people were telling him to get rid of me as a manager — and dump both Joe and I as band members. Jeff might have complained about us — behind our backs and to our faces — but he wouldn't do that.

Still, it didn't stop people from telling Jeff that he was naïve for sticking with us. And when you hear that stuff enough, you start to think about it. We'd gone to Hollywood as really good friends. We were still close when we left. But something changed. Everyone was a little bit more suspicious — of the world and of each other. The seeds of discontent stayed with us forever.

As a rapper once told me about the music business, "Dude, you are in the hood of no good."

As a rule, Jeff was not the type of guy who got excited about things. He liked being involved in the movie when we first started making it. But the thrill wore off after a few weeks. While Joe and I were gawking at the hot chicks and marveling over the visual aspects of filmmaking, Jeff wasn't feeling it.

Fortunately, though, all the distractions did nothing to diminish our music. That's why I have so much respect for Jeff and Joe. We were dropped into the middle of something, and we produced. I can't think of another band that could have been so prolific, given the exhausting schedule. For all my complaints about Hollywood, we were exposed to an outstanding crop of musicians who challenged us to raise our already high standards.

When we were cutting the Bob Dylan song "When the Night

Comes Falling from the Sky" I was having a rough time with the drumming. Everyone else was grooving, but I wasn't. I wouldn't say I sucked, but the drummer can make or break sessions, and this one was particularly hard for me. Remember — I wasn't an experienced recording drummer, and we couldn't afford to do anything halfway. So we made the decision to bring in Bobbye Hall, a female African-American percussionist who'd played on Bill Withers's "Lean on Me" as well as Pink Floyd's *The Wall*. Dylan, James Taylor and Carole King had all featured Bobbye on their albums. She gave the track exactly what it needed — and she did it pleasantly and without ego.

Bobbye put the music first. It was a lesson we all needed at the time.

The *Road House* soundtrack was released in conjunction with the movie, in 1989. Before our launch, we had a big meeting with Joel Silver, Clive Davis and Donnie Ienner, who'd later become Sony Music's chairman and is credited, along with Tommy Mottola, with turning Mariah Carey into a superstar. There were three mock-ups of the album art leaning against the wall, and the executives were all arguing: "It should be that one. It should be that one."

Suddenly, Jeff interrupted: "The one in the middle."

My eyes jumped from album cover to album cover. The one in the middle actually *was* the best one. The executives pondered the artwork, then looked at each other.

"Well, it *is* Jeff's band," somebody said. The decision was made.

I also want to point out that Jeff was very clear about the kind of album we were releasing. Because of his background and inspirations, *See the Light* was occasionally described as a blues album. "*See the Light* was not a blues album," he told *Guitar World* with exasperation. "There are a lot of rock and other music elements on it. A lot of people heard 'Blue Jean Blues' and 'Hideaway' and said, 'Aha — blues album!'"

Jeff knew that we'd made a rock album, and a commercial rock album at that — and didn't seem to have a huge problem with it. This is important because, later on, he would.

My maternal grandfather, Les Emin, who was decorated for fighting in the Battle of Vimy Ridge in World War I, with an army buddy. He was briefly a rumrunner before retreating to Yarmouth, Nova Scotia, where he became a respected family man and member of the community.

The park named for my grandfather and namesake, in Saint John, New Brunswick.

My mom, Rose, with (left to right) me, my sister Vivian and brother Wally.

Jeff with Stevie Ray Vaughan. CREDIT: TONY TOBIAS

Maybe the Stones couldn't get no satisfaction . . . but I sure did, meeting Charlie Watts.

The Jeff Healey and Bon Jovi bands with agent Steve Herman (right).

Give peace a chance.

A note of appreciation from the late, great George Harrison. What a gentleman!

Thanks for doing my song — I think you are an amazing guitarist Jeff — Love from George Harrison

To Tom Stephen
With best wishes,

Bill Clinton

Left to right: Ronnie Hawkins, President Bill Clinton, Wanda Hawkins, Jeff and me.

With Sam Wakim, my second father, and his good
friend Prime Minister Brian Mulroney.

This book might not have been written if my dear friend Susan, owner
of the Catcha Falling Star boutique hotel in Negril, Jamaica, hadn't
provided a sanctuary for co-author Keith Elliot Greenberg and me to
drill down. We are blessed in this world to have great friends.

Our first staff Christmas card.

Dutch festival.

Overnight, we went from being a bar band to being a big band. When *Road House* premiered in Canada, we couldn't even get our friends into the theater. There were klieg lights outside and police controlling the crowds. We were ushered in and sat down in the front row. Reporters were interspersed throughout the crowd, all trying to get to Jeff. He'd throw out a glib little line and they'd furiously scribble it down.

Gone were the days when we'd play two hundred-seat blues rooms. Now it was ten-thousand-seat arenas and fifty-thousand-seat stadiums. In the past, the three of us would carry our gear up the back stairs. Now we had other people to set up our equipment. We were too busy having our photos taken, doing interviews or talking about business.

It happened so fast.

Jeff described our circumstances in an interview with *Musician* magazine: "I hope I haven't changed too much more than what I naturally would in human evolution. I'm not one to get caught up in all the hype and the glamour and junk. I don't like the fact that to go into a major record store to do a little browsing, for instance, I have to call in advance to set it up.

"Well, let's not say I don't like it. Let's say I'm not used to it. But from the record company's marketing standpoint, that's the way it has to be. I have to meet the right people while I'm there, so they don't feel ignored. Otherwise, I'd just go in, grab some records and leave."

After Hollywood, I thought the road would be a sanctuary. That's where we were at our best, jamming onstage for our fans. But I'd still hear the same complaints over and over. *Jeff's too good for the rest of the band. Jeff needs a better manager.* At one point, I heard that Stevie Ray Vaughan's manager was the one generating some of this vitriol, and confronted him backstage. I was really pissed off and, when I saw the guy, I shoved him. He stumbled backwards and fell down the stairs.

I can't say I was sad, but I didn't want to kill the guy, either. When I saw him get up, I walked away, content that my point had been made.

Later, he threatened to sue me and charge me with assault. For whatever reason, he didn't.

Maybe he was afraid I'd do it again.

Finally, I sat down with Jeff and told him the rumors were getting to me. He assured me that I didn't have to worry. The Jeff Healey Band was like the Starship Enterprise, he said, "when the force field shields shut down and we're taking the hits. But it's all right, Tom. It's the three of us in the spaceship."

Sometimes, Jeff could make you the happiest guy in the world.

"I have a platinum record on my wall because of these guys," says Jonathan Clarke, the public relations executive Arista put in charge of hyping our band, who later became a popular New York radio disc jockey. Jonathan not only participated in some of our rock star adventures, he'd invite reporters along to partake, as well. "We were in New York at what used to be the Rihga Royal Hotel," he remembers, "and — I don't know what prompted it — Tom suddenly punched a wall and dented the Sheetrock. A writer was with us, and Tom looked at him and dared him to do the same thing. So he kicked the wall, and made the hole bigger. Then I kicked the wall and made the hole bigger, too.

"The next day, Arista got a phone call from the hotel. The bill was something like $1,300. I had to fess up about what happened, and thought I was going to be fired. But nothing really happened. I mean, Arista was seen as mainly a pop and R&B company — Whitney Houston, Aretha Franklin — and now the Jeff Healey Band had a hit with us, too. We knew that 'Angel Eyes' wasn't really representative of what Jeff was — a shredding, incendiary, blues guitar god — but everything was working. The relationships that Tom was forging at that time helped the band to continue to tour, make albums, get deals for their duration. A lot of doors were opening. People fell in love with Jeff Healey because he was so non-traditional, and he made such great television. When he played one of the late-night TV shows, people were talking about it the next day. There was no internet, so that's what you relied on.

"What helped the band was having that one big hit at the

beginning. And having that one big hit at the beginning is probably what hindered them later on."

One night, as we pulled up to a club, a large group of girls started pounding on our vehicle. "Look at all those girls banging on the windows," I observed.

"I'll have to take your word for it," Jeff quipped, "because I can't see them."

The truth is that — figuratively speaking — I barely saw them, either. All my energy had been devoted to pushing the label hard on "Angel Eyes." Since I always believed that we were fighting an uphill battle, I hadn't taken the time to realize how far we'd come. The promoter was sitting next to me and must have noticed the bewilderment in my eyes. "Yup, Tom," he said, "they're here for you guys."

"Fuck yeah!" I screamed. And the party started.

As much fun as we'd have at our scheduled gigs, the best times happened afterwards, when we'd find a little dive and jam with the local musicians. We were in this beat-up club in Little Rock one night when I spotted a distinguished-looking guy in the middle of the crowd who was obviously very important. There were two big dudes in shades on each side of him. When we were finishing up, someone ran up to me and said, "Excuse me, the governor would like to meet you all."

"The who?"

"The governor."

I wasn't sure what a governor actually did. "Is that like a premier in Canada?"

I was told that was an accurate comparison.

About 10 minutes later, we were talking with some people back-stage when in walked Bill Clinton. He was smiling from ear to ear and seemed to really love music.

"You boys are all a lot of fun," he said. "And Jeff, I've got to tell you. I never saw anything like you."

Jeff did that thing where he appeared to look Clinton in the eye. "Well, Guv, I have to say *I've* never seen anything like you."

We all had a laugh over that.

Always astute, Clinton had taken the time to learn about our background, and told us that he was friends with Ronnie Hawkins, the legendary Canadian bluesman.

"Well, I see you boys have a lot to do," he said before he left. "But one day, we'll all get together again. One day, you boys can come visit me at the White House."

With all the bullshit you hear in the music business, you learn not to take too many promises seriously. But a few short years later, Bill Clinton made good on his invitation.

CHAPTER
twelve ———————————

As soon as we had the movie out of the way, we started touring, more to support *See the Light* than the *Road House* soundtrack. And I don't mean a couple of weeks or even months on the road. We were traveling for the better part of two years. That's how the record company wanted it. There were a lot of people working to make the Jeff Healey Band well known, and it cost money to keep them on the payroll and retainer. If the machine stopped going, expenses went up. When the machine kept going, they stayed down. It's not that different than a cab driver who has to make sure that his vehicle is picking up fares 24 hours a day in order to generate a profit.

In one interview, Jeff spoke about the grind of the road. He estimated that he slept between three and five hours a night and, from 10 a.m. on, was dealing with media and other band-related business, eating breakfast and lunch while answering people's questions. "I'm not complaining," he said. "It's a hectic thing, something you have to be prepared for."

Whenever we arrived in a new place, I noticed that the assembled media treated us in general, and Jeff in particular, with a great deal of respect. Here's what I really admired about Clive Davis. He never wanted the band to be a circus act — *look at the blind kid and his guitar.* Clive understood the skill, the musicianship and the artistry — and that's the message that got sent to everyone who was marketing us around the world.

Most of our traveling took place outside of North America. The itinerary was largely the brainchild of Tony Tobias, who felt that we were increasing our fans' loyalty by becoming established far away from home. "I was negotiating publishing deals for the band, and I told them, 'Before you do America, you need to do Europe,'" he says. "'Because when America gives up on you and you're out of your deal, Europe will still be loyal. We can negotiate our own deals there, and you can go there for the next 20 or 30 years and play and play and play.' I mean, look at a band like the Ventures. When no one even knew who they were in the U.S. anymore, Japan still loved them 20 years later. So I told the guys, 'Let the people in these countries get to know you. They'll always want you back. That's the way it works. Trust me.'"

It certainly felt like we had a permanent home in England. The second we landed there, Jeff's picture was in the largest newspapers; the country was going nuts for him. Our first gig in London was at Ronnie Scott's Jazz Club, a storied London room where every great artist in the history of the business had played. It was a showcase, and all the superstars showed up — the who's who of the British music scene. And here we were, blowing it out onstage.

However, the sound was terrible. Each time Jeff hit his guitar, there was a horrible echo. It was driving Jeff crazy, but we managed to get through. Just like in Saskatoon, Boise and Moncton, people were blown away. *This guy's the real deal. He's the next coming of Hendrix.*

We did an encore then went backstage. Jeff didn't give a fuck about the praise. All he cared about was that awful echo. With so much at stake, he was as angry as I'd ever seen him. I wasn't feeling much better. We both wanted to punch somebody out when along came Bobby, our soundman. He was already drunk out of his mind. And he slurred, "Jeff, that was the best fucking *kitar* sound I've ever heard — ever!"

It was so ludicrous that Jeff and I began laughing. We forgot how pissed we were in the first place.

"Jeff was one of those guitar players who got the respect from everyone from Eddie Van Halen to the classic guys," says Stevie Salas. "In London, I remember going backstage and seeing Jeff sitting around with Jeff Beck and Gary Moore — I mean, the best in the world. And he didn't give a shit. He gave them no mind. One time, at an after-party for an awards show, these rock stars were lined up, hoping Jeff would invite them into his jam. And when he called me up onstage, everybody looked at me — because who am I? I'm nobody — like, 'You muthafucka, Stevie Salas.'"

Every morning, the reporters came one by one to pay homage to the new star. Jeff had answered most of the questions before. But he made each writer feel like he was being given a new, special insight. Why did Jeff hold his guitar on his lap? That's how he always did it, Jeff said. In his mind, he saw chord shapes when his hands touched the neck. It made him comfortable. It was his style.

How did the positioning of Jeff's instrument differ from that of sighted musicians? "I don't know," Jeff would respond. "I never saw a sighted musician play." Then he'd state that it didn't matter if you played with your feet. All that mattered was getting the song out.

When Jeff was asked why he was becoming popular in London, he'd say it was because he had so many relatives there. Then he'd pause and add, "Sorry. I thought you were talking about London, Ontario."

"The dumb questions are, 'You must listen to people like Ray Charles and Stevie Wonder to get inspiration,'" he told *Musician*

In London with Jeff Beck.

magazine. "That's dumb. The fact that they're blind and so am I is just that, a fact. But there are a lot of good musicians who can see, and a lot of blind guys who can't play a goddamned note. So the two have nothing in common as far as I'm concerned."

For a while, touring was great. Maybe they should have let us go home once in a while, but even now I wouldn't change it. Of course, the band members got on each other's nerves. We spent more time together than we'd probably ever spent with our parents or girlfriends. But 99 percent of the time we were laughing. We had our first album and the movie, and we had momentum.

Roadies are a very select community. Generally, these guys function on little or no sleep; they're hardcore partiers, and some of the most creative working people you'll meet. When you're a rock 'n' roll band, the roadies are the ones who pull the party together, introducing the girls. But don't worry — those guys are pretty good at looking after themselves, too. I've walked onto the tour bus a few times and seen some interesting sights.

A lot of the roadies who I knew ended up becoming road managers for major groups. The guys who are solely in it to chase the girls and get hammered don't last. Others become legends — guys musicians sit around and tell stories about. One time in Japan, a roadie — a fellow Maritimer named Mongo — was angry because the hotel was slow responding to his complaint about one thing or another. So he took apart the entire air-conditioning system.

As we traveled, we found ourselves in the company of models — fashion models, runway models, *Playboy* and *Penthouse* models. After we got over the novelty, I realized that some of the stereotypes about these girls were true. Not all of them were the sharpest. Some had been modeling since they were 13 or 14, and lived in a world so insular, they hadn't been exposed to the normal things that teenagers experience. Few of them took advantage of the cultural opportunities available when you travel to places like Paris and Rome and Amsterdam. By the time they were 19 or 20, they were veterans not only of wild sexual behavior but of heavy drinking, cocaine use and, well, partying with rock stars.

One well-known model whose name I won't mention was crazy about Jeff but had a bigger thing for coke and alcohol. She'd get blasted, then try to show up backstage before we'd go on. One thing about our band was that we had a rule: the music came first. No partying until after the show. However, this girl was so beautiful and famous that very few people said no to her. She took our decree as a personal insult.

One day, we gave strict instructions that this young lady was not to be allowed in the dressing room. Nevertheless, she managed to find her way backstage. She started bolting up the stairs and got to the top, where she ran directly into one of our larger security guards. The last thing we saw was him carrying her over his shoulder as she clawed at his back and slurred, "You can't do this to me! Don't you know who I am?! I'm a *purff-purff-pur*fessional model!"

A few years later, she went into rehab and relapsed a few times. Today her demons have been conquered. At the time, though, the sight of her being carried away was hysterical.

"Tom was in Spain and called me while I was in London," Stevie Salas says. "And I told him about these friends of mine who owned a modeling agency who were having a very exclusive dinner with all these supermodels. I was invited and so was Tom, so I told him, 'Come in tonight.' The problem was that Tom had promised his Spanish girlfriend a trip to London. 'Well, make up an excuse,' I said. 'You don't bring sand to the beach. You don't bring hamburger to a steak dinner.' But Tom didn't like going back on his word, so he brought along the girlfriend. She wasn't a supermodel. But she was hot, and also funny and cool. And soon, all the guys were hitting on her instead of the supermodels.

"The experience taught me something about Tom. He was as horny as the next guy. But he wasn't going to go back on his word just because something better came along."

I'm not sure that I was as sensitive as Stevie remembers. Like I've said, the Jeff Healey Band consisted of three nerds — nerds who were now making up for lost time with the ladies. And now we never had to play the aggressor. Jeff and I often had adjoining suites. One night in Denmark, I came to my room to find a girl tied to the bed.

"Where did this come from?" I asked myself.

I could hear snickering around a corner but didn't see anyone else.

"Tom, I've been waiting for you," the girl said.

At that moment, another girl came up behind me, and pulled me onto the bed for a threesome.

None of this would be happening, I thought, *if I didn't have a set of drumsticks.*

Jeff had obviously set up the whole thing. He couldn't watch. But he could listen, and I heard him giggling.

With all the action coming to us, Joe Rockman began thinking that he was a real lady killer, as I did to some extent. That was until an old blues player set us straight: "If Kermit the Frog was in this band, he'd be getting laid, too."

The guys who'd been on the circuit for much longer seemed

to have a balanced perspective on our situation. One time, Willie Nelson came on board the bus. Jeff was thrilled because he looked up to Willie as an incredibly talented singer-songwriter. As they engaged in small talk, Jeff asked, "Willie, tell me something I need to know."

Jeff was anxious for wisdom, hoping to learn something new about music. Instead, Willie said, "Jeff, I can tell you one thing for sure. Money and power makes women horny."

A couple of months later, we had a similar experience with Albert Collins. Rather than deliver advice himself, he told us a parable:

A college reporter finally has a chance to interview one of the great Black blues legends. He asks the gentleman, "Sir, what is it that makes you play music?"

"Son, it comes down to the three Ms."

The young, white college kid says, "Well, sir, please. What are the three Ms?"

The old man has a stutter. "The first M is *mu-mu*-music."

"Okay. I get that. What's the next one, sir?"

"The next M is *muh-muh*-money."

The young man says, "That's great. And what's the third one."

"The third M is the most important one. And it's *mmm-mmm-mmm-mmm*-pussy."

We told that joke for the rest of the tour. It was a different time.

"I've done some rock star shit in my life," says Stevie Salas. "My first band was Rod Stewart, and Rod taught me how to party. But I remember being with the Jeff Healey guys and ending up just with Tom and six gorgeous girls. Tom and I were sitting there and these girls were naked, all having sex with each other. I'm not going to say that Tom and I had our way with them. It was more like they let us in. We were pretty exhausted afterwards, too, having to service six women. But again, the girls were in charge. They just let us participate."

An old blues guy once told us, "You come out of a woman and you spend the rest of your life trying to get back into one." We were

Stevie Salas and me.

becoming successful at it, but the bad thing was that we began to believe that we could have anything we wanted whenever we wanted it. I cannot tell you how many times I'd just be walking down a hallway before a show when I'd get pulled into a room to be given a blow job. I'd stand there, and wonder if Jeff was getting impatient, waiting for me. Then the two of us would get together, and I'd learn that the exact same thing had just happened to him.

Sex aside, though, some of these ladies became friends. As fun and glamorous as the road could be, we were also tired, bored and lonely. The women we met were often a lot of fun, besides just being sexy. We'd go to the movies together, play cards or go bowling. I made a lot of good friendships and had a lot of good times, above the obvious attractions. In fact, many of these so-called groupies are still my friends today. Having them around often prevented the band from getting into stupid little arguments because we were burnt out and nitpicking.

But that didn't mean we didn't love each other's company. In

Paris, Jeff even walked with us a few flights up the Eiffel Tower. I don't know why; it's not like he could appreciate the panoramic view of the city of lights. Maybe he just wanted to hang out with us.

After our gig in Paris, Jeff called my room at three o'clock in the morning, and said, "All right. I'm jamming. Come play. The drummer here sucks. I need a drummer right now."

Then he hung up. But I was determined to find him. So I ran downstairs and started quizzing the cab drivers in front of the hotel. "Did anybody take a big blind guy somewhere?"

One driver remembered his friend shuttling Jeff someplace. This was before cell phones, so we couldn't contact the first driver. My guy told me to hop in his car, and he'd circulate through the area where the late-night music clubs were. We probably hit four places with no sign of Jeff. And then, as we rounded a corner, I heard the distinctive wail of Jeff's guitar coming down the street.

I ran into the club and pulled out my drumsticks, changing place with the drummer mid-song. As soon as I dug in, Jeff looked back, smiling. Whether he loved me or hated me on any given day, he knew my feel.

I found Paris incredibly charming. Aside from the music, though, Jeff wasn't impressed. Like many Canadians, I could understand some French. Jeff was an English-only guy. Even worse, he couldn't read visual signals when a French speaker was trying to make a point. His culinary tastes stopped at hamburgers and fries, so he wasn't very pleased when a top French label took us to one of the fanciest restaurants in the city and ordered seafood. As with sushi, Jeff was repulsed by the smell. And Joe was so spent from touring and partying that he literally fell asleep at the table.

On the way back to the hotel, Jeff and Joe asked our driver to pull over so they could load up on McDonald's. I don't know how this happened, but the head of the French label found out about our side trip and was personally offended. Were Jeff and Joe such savages that they'd snub a posh Parisian meal for such lowbrow American fare? From that point forward, we no longer had the label's support.

"I don't know if this is what you call success," Jeff complained to *Guitar Player* magazine in 1989. "Obviously, it's success, but we're not going to stop at this point. There will come a point when the three of us, with our other interests in life, will probably back off from the performing aspect for some time, or only do it for, say, one third of the year."

I wish I'd read that article at the time and followed Jeff's logic. We might have worn ourselves out a lot less. Even though most of our exhaustion was self-inflicted.

In Germany, two promoters were competing to bring us on tour. Both of them had hired former American military men who'd served in Germany; the Americans fixed problems and helped the some-times parochial-minded musicians from North America feel more at home. At some point, one of the promoters must have realized that we had a few days off; he invited me to Germany.

At the airport, I was met by Joe, a former Green Beret. He took me out to a killer dinner, then to a show where a girl fucked a dog. For once in my life, I felt prudish and left.

We had a chauffeured car, which next brought us to a large mansion. I said, "Where are we going, somebody's house?"

"No. It's a club. I think you'll like it."

We were admitted by two doormen carrying Uzis. I'd had a few drinks, and my attention immediately went to the bar. It was a beautiful deck from a boat, made of polished teak. As a sailor, I couldn't take my eyes off of it. "Look at this bar," I marveled to Joe.

"What the fuck is wrong with you?" he asked, nudging and pointing over his shoulder. "Look at that."

All the women in the place were wearing lingerie, garter belts and heels. I ended up in a bedroom with two of them. "Angel Eyes" happened to be playing on the radio, which enhanced the experience even more.

In the morning, I was taken to meet the promoter, who said all the right things. The Jeff Healey Band was not interested in short-term payoffs, and this guy had long-term plans about promoting us, year after year. Everything ended well, and I left Germany feeling optimistic.

But when I returned a few weeks later, Joe was at the airport, looking pissed off. Whatever money we made was automatically going to have $15,000 subtracted from the top, he said.

"Why?"

"Remember that mansion we went to? Do you think you're so attractive that those two girls are just going to bring you upstairs and fuck you for free? And that 'Angel Eyes' will just happen to be playing on the radio? And that they'd order bottle after bottle of champagne with their own money? They were professionals, Tom. We were trying to charm you, but we expected you to pay your bill."

I'd gotten so used to the rock 'n' roll life, I thought it had been just another night. Still, I refused on principle to pay the $15,000, and the promoter was willing to let it slide. I also told him I was in shock that I'd be exposed to something like this. After all, I was a Catholic!

And I must say, he did a pretty great job for us whenever we were in Germany, booking us on the massive Rock am Ring festival one year with acts like Bob Geldof, Dave Stewart, INXS and Sting.

The Berlin Wall had recently come down, and the country was experiencing growing pains reunifying. The promoter had a Russian associate in the formerly communist East who said he wanted us for a big festival. When we arrived, I saw this large, open field, but not much else. Jeff's instincts kicked in and he asked, "What's going on here? It seems kind of quiet. Something doesn't feel right."

Joe the former Green Beret and I walked over to the trailer that served as the production office. "Where is everybody?" I asked the Russian promoter.

"Other side of hill," he said in broken English. "Big campground. Thousands of people."

I went outside and commandeered a golf cart. At the top of the hill, I looked down. Nothing was there but a few speckled cows.

I delivered some instructions to our band and crew: "Only unload half the gear. Something doesn't look right. We play half a set. Short, sweet — and get out."

Back at the trailer, I confronted the Russian. "Unless those cows I saw have cash, how the fuck are you paying us?"

He apparently had forgotten how to speak English. But he began to lace into Joe the Green Beret in German, even opening his desk drawer at one point and showing off his gun. Joe had seen a few guns before and wasn't intimidated. He simply picked up the phone, called our main promoter in Germany and explained what was going on. Then he handed the phone to the Russian, whose tone turned contrite as he opened another drawer and began piling cash on the table. Not exactly what we were owed, but something.

Ultimately, about twelve hundred people turned up in a space that could have held thirty thousand. These were East Germans raised under the old system, very different from the modern, fashionable people we partied with in Munich and Frankfurt. This group was drunk, and the vibe was grouchy and ugly. We fulfilled our obligation and did the fastest load-out in the band's history.

As we were on the bus back to West Germany, I noticed a bunch of emergency vehicles speeding in the opposite direction with sirens blaring. We later found out that, after we left, the small crowd became ornery and tried to burn down the stage.

• •

During another European trip, we brought Ben Richardson along as a tour manager. There was a ten-day run of Italy planned, and the promoter, Sergio, met us at the airport. He was a nice guy with two competent assistants. What's strange was that there was another promoter, too, a Sicilian who we barely saw. We thought he was probably around because we were supposed to perform in Sicily at the end of the tour.

"After playing one show," Richardson says, "we were informed that the Sicilian date had fallen through, but the promoter would cover our hotel rooms in Rome for two days to make up for the lost gig. But every time I tried to get confirmation on this, I was getting the runaround. To make matters worse, the Sicilian had installed his wife, Rosa, as his representative. She was a middle-aged German who was grumpy all the time and the band quickly got sick of her. So, after talking with Tom, we decided — since Sergio was doing such a good job — to send the Sicilian and his wife home.

"When I called Sergio with the news, there was a long pause at the other end of the phone. 'Sergio,' I asked. 'Are you still there?'

"There was another pause, and then, he answered, 'Yes, I'm still here.'

"That's when I figured it out. 'Sergio,' I said, 'this Sicilian guy, is he mafia?'

"'Yes.'

"'And you're scared of him, right?'

"'Yes.'

"Since I wasn't ready to die yet, I told Tom about the situation, and we phoned the Sicilian to say the whole thing had been a misunderstanding, we were happy to have Rosa around and everything was great. The rest of the tour was a lot of fun, ending with a huge concert in front of fifty thousand people. Robbie Krieger and John Densmore from the Doors were the headliners. Before they went on, they mentioned to us that they almost cancelled the date, since the Sicilian had tried to promote them as the Doors, in violation of their contracts. Both Tom and Jeff were big fans of the Doors and, when Tom heard this, he became irate.

"Right there, he called the Sicilian and started screaming at him on the phone. 'This is Tom Stephen. Not only are you trying to screw us, but you tried to screw Robbie Krieger and John Densmore. Fuck you! You're a fuckin' asshole!'

"The guy had balls of steel. We ended up paying for our hotel in Rome, where I hid, scared shitless for two days."

Maybe I should have been more nervous, but I loved Rome and the people we met there. Jeff and I ended up jamming in a little blues bar on a side street, where the owner brought us into his wine cellar and let us taste his private collection. At 5 a.m., the owner and I ended up inside the Roman Coliseum, watching the sun come up. It was a sobering experience to stand in the middle of that history. The one image that stands out is the sight of hundreds of cats, scurrying around the ruins. Apparently, they hunt for rats in the Coliseum, like lions chasing the ancient Christians. A few days later, when I was back in Toronto, I opened my luggage and discovered two bottles of homemade wine.

The owner had taken it on himself to leave me with this very generous gift. I wish I could remember his name so I could thank him for his hospitality.

In Australia, we amused ourselves one day by going to a large indoor Go-Kart track on the Gold Coast. To keep Jeff on course, our roadie Chris tethered their Go-Karts together. While the rest of us were flying, Jeff and Chris were moving kind of slow.

"Fuck this," Jeff commanded. "Untie this goddamn Go-Kart."

Jeff planted his foot on the gas. He banged into shit and had to back up a few times, but so what? Without anyone to guide him, he made it around the track twice.

Japan was one of the more interesting places we toured. The audiences were fantastic and completely engaged in everything we did. But they tended not to clap. This was unnerving to Jeff. We'd play the first song. Nothing. Second song. Nothing. Third song. Still no reaction, as far as Jeff could gauge.

"Man, what's going on?" he'd ask. "These guys hate us. Is anyone even alive out there?"

"Yeah, Jeff, it's okay. Everyone's watching us. No one left. I guess we must be doing something right."

Then we'd get to the end of the show, and the place would go crazy, repeatedly chanting, "Encore! Encore!"

Japan was where Jeff started to fall in love with Squier guitars. Gary, our roadie, was already a fan, and added a specially wrapped pickup, which gave Jeff a much better sound.

While we were visiting Japan, we stayed at a boutique hotel with a bunch of metal guys: I think it was White Snake, Jake E. Lee and Poison. The girls who showed up couldn't distinguish one group from the other. As long as you looked like a Western rock 'n' roller — with the cowboy boots, long hair and tight T-shirt — that was good enough for them. I'd literally have them knocking on my door, two or three at a time.

Our hotel had an atrium extending about six floors up, and while I was in the room, I could hear an echo and some kind of splashing noise. I opened my door and saw Jeff leaning against the balcony rail with one of our roadies. "What the hell is going on?" I asked.

Jeff motioned me forward. The groupies were coming out of the different bands' rooms, stripping naked and jumping — past our floor — off the balcony into the pool at the bottom of the atrium. That's how I remember it anyway. I thought it was funny — until I learned that the hotel intended to charge the bands fifty dollars for each towel the girls used.

The same night, one of the roadies thought it would be amusing to hit me with a blast of a fire extinguisher. I knew it was all in jest, but it still pissed me off. I began chasing him until he dropped the extinguisher, ran into his room and locked the door.

Always the supreme instigator, Jeff taunted me: "You're just going to let him get away with that shit?"

That was all the incentive I needed. Holding the extinguisher, I began beating on the door. Incrementally, with each blow, the device fused the steel door to its frame, welding the roadie into his room.

Between the price of the towels, the door, all the drunken phone calls that the band members made back to Canada, and a government scam exit tax, we barely broke even. But no one could say we didn't enjoy ourselves.

• •

Back in Canada, MuchMusic had a program called *Mike & Mike's Excellent X-Canada Adventures*, featuring hosts Mike Rhodes and Mike Campbell touring the country by train with various rock acts. The only drawback was that the sponsor, Diet Pepsi, specified that its product was the only ingredient allowed to be mixed into the drinks in the bar car. Even so, the trip felt like a victory lap around the country, allowing us to stop into the clubs where we started and sit in with the local bands.

"Everyone got along," cohost Mike Campbell says. "The band wasn't sick of each other yet, and my cohost, Mike Rhodes, was even able to laugh it off when Tom and I stole the key to his room in Edmonton, then called the front desk to say that some crazy fan was going around claiming to be Mike Rhodes, and under no circumstances should he be given a room key.

"On the train, Jeff had to use a braille deck of cards. Of course, with his memory, he remembered the feel of every card and won every hand. So I had the cameraman rig up a small camera on a hockey stick and hold it over Jeff's shoulder. He might not have been able to see, but he was smart enough to know we were cheating. How else could it be that he was suddenly starting to lose?"

Steve Anthony, a MuchMusic VJ from 1987 to 1995 — and later host of the Toronto morning show *CP24 Breakfast* — once handed Jeff a regular set of cards during the train tour. When Jeff protested,

Mark Caporal.

Steve yelled, "I don't give a shit. Fuck you. I'm sick of you beating the shit out of everybody."

"There was nothing more significant to pop music in Canada at that time than MuchMusic," Steve says. "A lot of what we did was cheesy, but it hadn't been done before, so everyone thought it was cool. Canadian culture had been very regional, and MuchMusic joined the country from coast to coast. Someone who might have heard a Jeff Healey Band song on the radio could now watch a video and go, 'Wow, he's one of the greatest guitarists on the planet.' Then they'd see an interview segment, where he'd be playing cards with me on the train. And they'd say, 'Well, he happens to be blind, and he's funny and smart and sarcastic. If they put him up on a pedestal, it was because they knew Jeff as a person as well as a musician.

"Jeff would jog through the cars of the train without any help, making fast rights, fast lefts, as if he had sight. You thought he was going to hit a wall, but he never did. One of the coolest moments for me was riding through the Canadian Rockies in a freight car, with the doors open and the breeze going in, with the Jeff Healey Band jamming. It was exactly what rock 'n' roll was supposed to be."

There's a sad addendum to this story. The reason we appeared on MuchMusic in the first place was because Mark Caporal, a music executive who'd been a drummer in the band Eye Eye, had seen us play live and dragged Mike Campbell — his friend and roommate — to a show. It was through his work at the Canadian performance rights organization, SOCAN, that we received our first advance. He remained a supporter until 1991, when he accepted a job at EMI Music Publishing. Just before the gig started, Mark — an experienced pilot who owned his own plane, an Aeronca Champ — decided to take his first glider ride. Unfortunately, in the course of the journey, the instructor had a heart attack and fell forward onto the stick. The plane flew into the ground, and Mark died in the crash.

I'd like to be philosophical and say death is part of life, but that one really sucked.

• .

In Halifax, we went to one of my favorite local spots, the Midtown Tavern. Jeff loved the place because you could have a steak and beer and hang out with the people who'd supported us when the band was starting out.

I showed up with a Danish model I'd met in Japan. There was also a large contingent of guys I'd known from high school and university, all marveling over the fact that I'd been in a major motion picture and returned with one of the most beautiful young women on earth.

Jeff was racking up points playing shuffleboard. As usual, people were challenging me: "What's going on, Tom? This is some kind of gimmick. How can a blind guy be kicking our ass at shuffleboard?" But it was just Jeff being Jeff.

I went to use the washroom — well, to be completely honest, I disappeared into the washroom to do some coke with a friend — and when I got out, most of the people had left. I thought it was strange that they hadn't waited to say goodbye. And I noticed that Jeff was waiting for me, gulping beer and snickering.

"So how's it going, big shot? Good to be home?"

My Danish girlfriend approached and told me in her broken English, "All of your friends were wonderful, and they wanted me to tell you they had a really great time, and no matter who you think you fuckin' are, they'd like to thank you very much."

I was then handed a tab for everybody's steak and drinks — a total of a couple thousand dollars.

Actually, it was a great lesson. I might have been the conquering hero, but my buddies were letting me know to keep my feet on the ground and not be a jackass. Because things were good today, but who knew what tomorrow would bring?

thirteen

The three nerds were doing pretty well for ourselves. After selling three hundred thousand copies in Canada, *See the Light* went platinum in the United States. In the land we'd dreamed of conquering, people bought a million albums — half of what we sold worldwide at the time.

When the awards ceremonies came around, we received nominations in all of them: the Junos in Canada, the *Billboard* Music Awards, the World Music Awards. In 1988, our single "Hideaway" received a Grammy nomination for Best Rock Instrumental. Every time we landed somewhere, we'd turn on the radio and hear "Angel Eyes" or "Confidence Man."

Of course, we were ecstatic. But when Jeff was interviewed, he'd play it humble. "I really don't dwell on it," he told *Canadian Musician* about the accolades and honors. "People who focus on compliments are usually insecure regarding their playing to begin with. The bottom line is you yourself have to know what you're capable of."

What he wasn't saying was that the nonstop interviews could be a pain in the ass, especially when someone was translating all the questions from Flemish or Portuguese or Italian and Jeff was having a hard time understanding the accent. The translators did try to make the process easier with visual cues, sometimes strumming an imaginary guitar on their laps — like so many others, after spending a few minutes with Jeff, they had

On The Tonight Show Starring Johnny Carson.

forgotten that he couldn't see. And given his sometimes pedestrian tastes, he'd get mad when he'd sit down and order a hamburger, only to be told he had to choose from *goulash*, *fischbrötchen* and *hasenpfeffer*.

Sometimes a new tour date would come up that one of us wouldn't want to take and the others would. Or there'd be a meet and greet when we just wanted to go to the room and sleep for a week. No one was going to blow off the fans and skip it, but once the novelty of being famous wore thin, we weren't always having the time of our lives.

This was particularly true when we'd all be hanging out in a hotel suite and I had to get up to make a business call to another continent. No one had cell phones, of course, so that meant I'd leave the party, lock the bedroom door and wait an hour or so for the operator to connect me. Then, after everyone had had a good time trashing me for ditching them to talk business, I'd have to come back out and deliver news that the band — or at least, Jeff — wasn't in the mood to hear. So I was starting to be perceived as the bad guy.

But what fuckin' choice did I have? We were a bona fide commodity now — a machine, as far as the record company was concerned, and they wanted more product. Because we spent so much time on the bus, going from date to date, we were one of the first bands to build an automotive music studio, with drums and gear and recording rigs. But between the reporters, the girls, the booze and the fatigue, we barely used it. With all the idle time we spent together, we could have written enough material for the next half century. Yet I hardly remember coming up with any songs at all.

The environment was just too superficial and confining for a wide-open musician like Jeff. He didn't want to sit on a bus and rehearse, and there was no room for him to leap out of his chair and jump all over the place. "My practice comes from getting out with other people and playing on stage," he told the British magazine *Guitarist*. "I work very much with an on-the-spot, spur-of-the-moment kind of thing." *See the Light*, for instance, had been a "transformation over the last couple of years, but not anything that I could actually point out. It just started one way and, over hundreds of times of playing it, it gets a little different."

It was a wonderfully inspiring story about the gestation of a debut album. But now that the Jeff Healey Band was known we needed something more than that to keep the public interested.

The longer we stayed on the road, the less we smelled the roses and the more we felt the thorns. On airplanes, Jeff usually put on his headphones and closed everyone else out by listening to old-school jazz. But on one particular flight to Amsterdam, he was unusually talkative. We were flying at about thirty-five thousand feet and he said, "When you think about it, up here, we are closer to God or, at least, closer to heaven."

"Jeff," I replied, "you're talking to the wrong guy. You want to go with height, relative to heaven, I get it. But when I look up, I don't think of heaven. It's when I look down that I feel things like that. I mean, man, this planet is amazing."

Jeff's mood changed. "When you look down, you think of heaven. I think about how humans are going to fuck the whole thing up."

Another time, driving through the Rockies, Joe looked out the window and just marveled at the wildlife, the trees and the mountains. "Isn't it beautiful?" he asked.

"How the fuck would I know?" Jeff shot back. "You know what traveling's like for me? I get to the airport. I go up. I go down. I wait around. That's it."

The poor guy was bored, just living in his head most of the time.

"We were at this beautiful theater in British Columbia before a show," said Bret Gallagher, who later became president of southern California for Live Nation. "My brother, Dan, was a Canadian television personality, and he was trying to explain to Jeff what the theater looked like. But after a few seconds, he realized Jeff wasn't really that interested. So he just said, 'What the fuck am I bothering explaining this to you? You're never going to get to see it anyway.' And Jeff laughed. If you just told him, 'That's the way it is,' he appreciated it."

In addition to the road-weariness, the gossip that had started in L.A. never abated. In fact, the more places we visited, the more people Jeff met who tried to convince him that the band needed some alterations — and they knew exactly what needed to be done. Usually, that involved ditching Joe and me, and hiring them. Compounding this whole thing was the fact that Jeff was a jazz guy, and the jazz snobs were constantly telling him that the Jeff Healey Band wasn't producing real music. To his credit, Jeff seemed to know that most of these self-appointed advisors were trying to grab a piece of what we'd all worked so hard to build. But when you begin hearing this kind of argument on a monthly, weekly or sometimes a nightly basis, things can never be the same as they were before. In very subtle ways, I noticed Jeff withdraw.

After our tour ended, we took a six-month hiatus. Jeff was sick of the wear and tear, and sick of us. We needed to get away from each other and recharge.

In 1989, we were back in the studio, working on our next album, *Hell to Pay*. Arista claimed to be 100 percent in our corner. But it was no secret that the label wanted us to come up with another "Angel Eyes." Now that we'd had the crossover success, that became the standard that the record company expected; we were in a world where we had to have hits on pop radio. And that was really tough on Jeff, who had the heart of a jazz man and refused to live and die over whether other people considered him a radio star. "See the Light" had been on rock radio, but he never asked for that. Same with "Confidence Man." And "Confidence Man" was a song Jeff didn't even write; John Hiatt did. So I think our stardom, and the way we were perceived because of it, was a disappointment to Jeff.

It all went back to the way he grew up. In Jeff's house, everything was about country music, which is predicated on chords, structure and melody. He never understood the "cool" factor in rock 'n' roll and, honestly, didn't want to. And here I was, trying to be the middleman between Jeff and the record company. When I wasn't with the guys, I was rolling with the big shots and producers, who looked at the band as a moneymaker. So many other people had their futures hitched to our wagon that we were all feeling the pressure. We were a business, and everything that we did was being scrutinized.

"Tom and I were in a stretch limo, going to an awards ceremony," Mike Campbell from the *Mike & Mike* television show remembers. "Tom was used to traveling like this, but my partner, Mike Rhodes, and I weren't. We'd been partying all night, but now it was a new day, and Tom needed to call someone from Arista in New York. Let's remember that this was a long time ago, and calling from a car was an exotic thing. I was amazed that Tom just picked up the handset in the limo and dialed a number. Apparently, the label guy had some issues with the budget he'd been presented with. It started out with the usual pleasantries — 'Hey, man, how's it going?' and that sort of thing — followed by Tom saying, 'Yeah, everything's great here, but let's talk about the video.' There was a long pause while Tom listened to the New York guy and I could see him moving around in his seat, clearly becoming agitated. Then Tom chimed in and his voice was rising. He was getting pissed off. After a few back-and-forths, Tommy suddenly thrust the phone in front of his face and yelled into it, 'With all due respect, go fuck yourself,' and hung up. Startled, and a little bit embarrassed because I'd just listened to a private conversation, I looked right at him. 'What did you just do?' He laughed. 'I'm just making the point that we know better than that guy does about a video that's going to get played in Canada first.' He waited about five minutes and phoned the guy back.

"The second conversation again, ended with Tommy slamming the phone in the car down after another emphatic, 'With all due respect, go fuck yourself.'"

Our studio for the *Hell to Pay* project was outside of Montreal, in Morin-Heights. It was just like the old days, waking up in the middle of nowhere to six-foot snowdrifts. It was the three of us together again — without the record guys and the hangers-on. There was a really cool club about 20 miles away in Sainte-Adèle, Quebec, that we'd try to get to on the weekends. You had the elites of Montreal hanging out, and tons of girls, and the manager just gave us the run of the place. One night, I was driving there through the snow when the cops pulled me over and put me in handcuffs. Apparently, I fit the description of a bank robber. By the time we got to the police station, though, the officers had figured out that they had the wrong guy.

"We think you're just a drunk," one of them told me.

"No argument there."

Jeff and Joe thought the story was pretty funny. For most of the time, though, *Hell to Pay* was a tense record to make. We didn't come in with any real music that was ready to go, just a couple of ideas. Jeff was there in body but not necessarily mind and spirit. Fortunately, he was so good that no one else would have noticed. In the studio, he'd drill down, do his bit and make some killer songs.

What was happening at the time was that Jeff wasn't getting a lot of love for his writing from Arista. Clive always spoke to Jeff in a reasonable, respectful way. But in his autobiography, *The Soundtrack of My Life*, Clive admitted that he wasn't overly impressed with the band's writing. "He (Jeff) didn't write the hits on his platinum album debut . . . or on the *Road House* soundtrack," Clive wrote, "but when it came to doing the all-important second album, he demonstrated stronger resistance to outside material."

When it was time to write that next big single, Arista wanted to bring in ringers to help us out. This type of control was typical of Arista. Whitney Houston had apparently had some of her material rejected by the label because it was "too Black-sounding." But when she released the songs that the company wanted, some African-Americans condemned her as a "sellout," striking a deep nerve. Barry Manilow briefly left the label after arguing that the songs that he was given — including his biggest hits — had nothing to do with his true personality.

I was in the awkward position of trying to keep the balance between the band and Arista, and probably could have done a better job. I felt loyal to Jeff since he was the leader of our band, but was also trying to see our future from a management perspective. The whole process was kicking me in the ass. Clive wanted us to realize our full potential and, with a few more hits, we could have been elevated to Clapton status. But he should have been more encouraging of Jeff's writing, and I should have spoken up for him. In the meantime, I tried to sell Jeff on the concept of collaborating with outside writers: "Look, don't feel slighted. This is a way to improve your skills. Work with some of these great writers — cowrite with them. Master the craft. There's a whole other future there for you, another way to stretch your abilities as a musician. Clive knows what he's doing. It's not really a problem . . ."

"Yeah," Jeff replied. "But it kind of sucks."

"It was a tricky situation," says former Arista A&R executive Mitchell Cohen. "Most of the time, you talk to a manager to get him thinking your way, so he can reason with the band. But Tom

ARISTA RECORDS, INC.
Arista Building
6 West 57th Street
New York, N.Y. 10019
(212) 489-7400

<u>VIA STANDARD AIR</u>

CLIVE DAVIS
PRESIDENT

October 3, 1989

Dear Jeff:

Mitchell Cohen and I have gone over a lot of Tony Joe White material. Don't get scared now, but we have come up with three really strong songs that are hard to ignore. Naturally, we don't expect you to record all three but I have to personally go on record to say that these are real quality pieces of material and if they were properly arranged and produced, hit singles could result from any one of them without a compromise of any artistic integrity. So, we're sending you three in one package and looking to your feedback on each.

Warm regards,

Clive

w/encl:

As you can see, Clive thought our songwriting could be enhanced by some outside assistance.

145

was *in* the band, and the band was a very tight circle. What I tried to emphasize was that it doesn't matter whether or not Eric Clapton wrote, 'I Shot the Sheriff.' When you hear 'I Shot the Sheriff,' you say, 'It's an Eric Clapton song.'"

As much as Arista may have knocked Jeff's songwriting abilities, those skills were pretty pronounced on the album. He'd go off for a few days and come up with some gems. He wrote "Something to Hold On To" alone. And the title track, "Hell to Pay," as well as "Highway of Dreams" and "Life Beyond the Sky," were all written by the three of us.

I can't speak for Joe, but I'm the last guy who *should* have been writing a song for this album. Just being Jeff Healey's drummer was challenging enough. But we were trying to get something going, and if I needed to be a songwriter in addition to the drummer and management, then that's what I was going to be. I wouldn't say writing alongside Jeff was always easy, but it was extremely satisfying. Especially because Jeff believed we had something to prove. Once Jeff was told he couldn't do something, he went at it harder. And he pulled us up to the level that enabled us to write some decent material.

One of the writers directed to us was Bobby Whitlock, a Clapton associate who was involved with composing six tracks on *Layla and Other Assorted Love Songs* and sang backup vocals with Eric on George Harrison's *All Things Must Pass*. Being around a musician of Bobby's caliber was a dream. And he was a cool guy and loved hanging out with us as much as we liked being with him. In spite of this, our collaboration didn't yield any solid songs. It's hard to say why — except maybe we were all having a little too much fun.

Regardless, we were able to rely on some of our favorite songwriters to help give the album the right edge. Steve Cropper and Little Jimmy Scott's "How Long Can a Man Be Strong" brought out the bluesman in Jeff. And John Hiatt's "Let It All Go" received a good deal of airplay.

The exposure we got from *Road House* and *See the Light* put us in an enviable position. Some of the biggest names in rock 'n' roll were clamoring to collaborate with us. Over the last few years, I'd gotten to know Mark Knopfler's manager, Ed Bicknell — a very cool guy who also happened to be a drummer. For whatever reason, Dire Straits wasn't interested in recording Knopfler's song "I Think I Love You Too Much." It was a brilliant track. Not only did Mark give us the song, but he recorded a portion of it, playing his heart out and singing these high harmonies in the back end. Just incredible stuff. But when it came time for us to add our tracks, Jeff wanted to make changes.

After the mix was completed, you couldn't hear Knopfler's guitar solo at all, and barely make out the background vocals. When I questioned Jeff's judgment, he accused me of being starstruck.

"But Jeff," I countered, "he wants to be in our video."

"What do we need Mark Knopfler in our video for? We're the Jeff Healey Band."

This really pissed me off. "Jeff, I don't know if you're blind when it comes to sight or blind when it comes to promotion. How is it that one of the best self-promoters I know can't see the value of having Mark Knopfler in his video?"

"The song's staying the way it is," Jeff said with finality.

Now, some might argue that Jeff made "I Think I Love You Too Much" into a better song. I truly think this is what Jeff believed. And he also wanted to protect the reputation of the band. But he wasn't looking at the long-term consequences. Jeff was turning Mark Knopfler into an adversary. And that was bad for the Jeff Healey Band, since Dire Straits was one of the biggest bands on the planet.

The plan was for Knopfler to appear in the video we were going to shoot when we were in London, performing at Albert Hall. Gratis. But, first, I sent the song over to Ed Bicknell.

When he called back, he immediately affected a very British type of irritated politeness. "Tom, just a question. The mix you sent us — is that the final mix?"

"Well . . ."

"Right. It sounds quite lovely, but where's Mark's part?"

I had no choice but to lie. "Actually, we're remixing it as we speak."

It cost us several hundred grand to cross the ocean, in addition to production fees, but no one cared that much because we were making a video with Mark Knopfler. On the day of the shoot, though, we found ourselves sitting around the studio, waiting for him to show up.

When I tracked down his manager, he apologized, but said that Mark was on the other side of London at a soccer game, and there was ungodly traffic. "Oh, you English with your football," I joked. "If it wasn't for rock 'n' roll, you'd all be soccer players. Sit tight. I'll come up with a plan."

Immediately, I phoned Arista in New York and asked for authorization to rent a helicopter.

"No problem," I was told. "Just get him in the video."

Feeling relieved, I told the manager my solution. We'd find a spot near Knopfler, bring him to the studio, then fly him wherever he wanted to go. "The flight's maybe 15 minutes, tops," I said. "The whole thing won't be more than an hour. Where do you want us to pick him up?"

"Right. Let me get back to you on that."

Five minutes passed, then 10, then 30. I was in a bit of a panic but tried not to show it when I called the manager again. This time, he said that Mark wasn't "really into helicopters."

As I tried to come up with a better alternative, he quickly added, "I'm not sure Mark's going to be able to make it."

At that point, I knew I was fucked. So I asked, "What's really going on?"

This time he didn't bother with any niceties. "What's really going on is one of the greatest songwriters in the world in one of the biggest bands in the world gave you a fuckin' song and you turned down his bloody fuckin' parts. I can't help but think that you blokes are three fuckin' idiots."

I have to admit, I saw his point.

A year or so later, we ran into Knopfler again when we both appeared on the same television show. We were supposed to play "I Think I Love You Too Much." But Knopfler got his revenge by playing the song solo first, leaving us scrambling to find another track.

Still, there was an even bigger name who I discovered was interested in lending his eminence to *Hell to Pay*. We'd always covered "While My Guitar Gently Weeps" in our shows, and Clive thought that it had great potential for a single. So I decided to push my luck. "Well," I told him, "you're Clive Davis. You know how to make things happen. Can you get George Harrison to play on our single?"

Not only was George known for writing the song, but Clapton had played that famous solo on the original recording. I was imagining Harrison and Jeff in the studio, confident that our version might be a little better.

One night, after playing drums all night, I went back to the band house while Joe and Jeff finished up in the studio. At about 4 a.m., the phone rang. On the other end was a fellow with a British accent, asking for me.

"Who's this?"

"It's George Harrison."

I rolled my eyes. Jeff fancied himself as a mimic, but I actually thought he was putting the accent on a little too thick. "Jeff," I said, "stop fucking around," and hung up.

A minute later, the phone rang again. This obviously wasn't the first time someone had mistaken a call from a former Beatle for a prank. George was laughing and managed to convince me that this was no joke.

"Is my accent really that bad?"

"Oh my God. I'm sorry."

He spoke about his admiration for Jeff, and really touched me when he said, "And to be clear, I think you guys are a fantastic rhythm section."

I mean, *Christ!* If that doesn't make you feel good, nothing will.

"Now, Tom, I can't come to Canada. I'm in Hawaii at present, but I'm flying back home through L.A. I'll only be there a couple of hours but, if you like, I'll be the studio with Jeff Lynne, and we can work on the song together."

"Of course, Mr. Harrison."

"No, Tom. 'George' is fine."

The second I got off the phone, I called the studio. "Look," I told the guys, "George Harrison is going to phone shortly and, for Christ's sake, don't hang up on him like I did."

Jeff was incredulous. "Go to sleep. We have a big day later on."

"No, Jeff, you don't understand. This is real."

Jeff later told me that he also slammed the phone down when Harrison called the studio. I believed this until I was researching this book — and a witness revealed that Jeff had invented that part of the story just to laugh at my reaction.

I sent our "slaves" — or the tracks we'd played on — to L.A. Then George and Jeff Lynne added their parts. Afterwards, Jeff received a lovely letter from George with a personal phone number, leaving the door wide open for future collaborations. Yet, once again, when it came time for the mix, Jeff turned George all the way down, triggering alarms in my head.

"Jeff, for God's sake. This is a Beatle."

"Well, I'm not a Beatle. I'm Jeff Healey of the Jeff Healey Band."

"I know, Jeff, but this is George Harrison. And look what he did for us."

"His part doesn't even fit where it is."

"Jeff, we're going to get a pretty bad reputation if we keep doing stuff like this."

Jeff would have none of it. As with Knopfler, he believed that he was improving the track. To Jeff, he was only doing what was best for the band. It wasn't until years later, when I was remixing the song for some reissues, that I was able to bring up George's voice in the mix. Just thinking about it now gives me chills. It's eerie to hear the beautiful sounds of Jeff and George soloing back-to-back. It's as if the two of them are standing just a few feet away from me. Yet I know that they're both dead — literally angels of rock 'n' roll.

CHAPTER
fourteen

As soon as *Hell to Pay* was released, we were back on the road, supporting the record. Like the previous tour, this one was international and nonstop.

A lot of bands wanted to tour with us but, after some discussion, we chose to open for Bonnie Raitt. "We were considering Fleetwood Mac," Joe told the magazine *Performance*. "We were considering a lot of other tours that are going on out there. But this one has a lot of credibility and, stylistically, it's a good marriage."

It was a choice that took some thinking. "We were hesitant at first," Joe said, "because we are trying to present the band as growing more in a rock direction. We've been fighting this typing as a blues band for so long. We were wondering if doing the Bonnie Raitt tour might just peg us back into the blues vein, which is something we really don't want to have focused on us so much. But right now, she's in the mainstream." In fact, after knocking around for some 20 years, Bonnie's 10th album, *Nick of Time* was at the top of the U.S. charts. "She's got a lot of dedicated, loyal fans and now, hopefully, she's got a whole lot of new, young fans, which we cater to, also."

I'm not sure Jeff would have approved of Joe's nakedly commercial motives; truthfully, I wasn't completely comfortable riding the line between blues and the so-called "hit radio" world. But, in the same article, Jeff noted that the band was maturing — musically, if not personally. "It's kind of hard to describe until you hear it, but there's a growth to the band's music. The quality is a little better. The performances are a little better."

In some ways, the partnership with Bonnie seemed like a mismatch. She was such a big star that we were regularly playing in venues that held twenty-five thousand people. Generally, our instinct in those situations was just to rock the joint. Fortunately, Jeff knew how to read an audience's vibe. He understood that it wouldn't work if we blew the place up and then segued into a mellower Bonnie show. So we'd focus on "Angel Eyes" and some of our slower stuff. "Just because you have a Marshall Stack," Jeff said, "doesn't mean you have to turn it up to 14."

And just because I had 5B sticks didn't mean I had to go out and put holes in the drums. You win more people over by respecting the dynamics in the place where you've chosen to play. "I'm there to entertain," Jeff said in one interview. "So I have to play the audience by ear. The first couple of tunes I try to deliver. Then, you sort of feel them out. If the audience is with you, the whole energy is so different."

Later on, a lot of people would tell me that they considered *Hell to Pay* our best album. It was definitely a strong record, and the reviews were very good. Nobody slammed us. If you're going to be dismissed as a fad, people come swinging at your second record. We survived the scrutiny.

When *Hell to Pay* was released in 1990, it sold exceptionally well in Europe and was one of the top albums in Canada, winning a Juno nomination for Album of the Year in 1991. That's not bad for a sophomore album. "While My Guitar Gently Weeps" was a good tune, and people responded to it positively worldwide. But I didn't get the sense that that was what the record company was looking for. We didn't have that one, big single like we did on the first album.

Because of *See the Light*, we were victims of high expectations. As a rule, blues guys can barely sell fifty thousand records. Had we hit two hundred thousand on the first album, everyone would have been happy. But because we'd sold in the millions, there was disappointment with *Hell to Pay*. We did our job. I'm not sure the promotion people did theirs. Instead of really pushing our singles, I think they hung back, waiting for the record to sell itself.

A lot of changes were happening in music at this time. Grunge was hitting, and rap stars were taking over the world. In that environment, it was easy to get overlooked. We were good — no one disputed that — but we weren't the band everybody *had* to hear.

The great thing about being a musician, though, is that the second you hit the stage, none of that other shit counts. It doesn't matter if you've been battling with the record company, bickering on the bus or doing interviews for the last 12 hours. When the music starts, it recharges you.

Grammy-nominated producer and composer Mischke was one of our supporting vocalists on the *Hell to Pay* tour. In 1993, he remembers, "We were opening up for Bon Jovi, and we were in Montreal at the Forum. It wasn't the biggest place we played on the tour, but it was definitely the loudest place I've ever played in my life. They lost it for Jeff. Even though we were the opening act, he was Canadian, and he put on one hell of a show. That night, every one of us said the same thing. Our ears were ringing not from the volume on the stage, but from the people. And we played huge festivals in Europe with a hundred thousand people. I've never heard applause like that. Ever."

Yet, Jeff was always aware of how fickle life could be, and was deeply affected by Stevie Ray Vaughan's unexpected death in 1990. What made it even more tragic was that, a few days earlier, we'd met

Stevie Ray hanging out back at the hotel.

up with Stevie, Eric Clapton and Robert Cray on tour. First, Jeff joined Clapton on stage for a killer version of "Crossroads." For the encore, Jeff returned, and he, Clapton, Stevie Ray and Cray launched into a wicked rendition of "Sunshine of Your Love," I flashed back to my days playing the song in my garage. It was only natural to ask myself, "How the fuck did I get here, surrounded by these greats?"

It was a high point for everybody. And just like that, it switched.

On August 27, 1990, Stevie was leaving a gig in Wisconsin. Clapton's crew had rented a helicopter, but Stevie was anxious to get to Chicago and was given the last seat. At 1 a.m., the chopper crashed into the side of a 300-foot ski slope, killing everyone on board.

What made it worse was a press report that claimed that Jeff and Eric Clapton were also on the helicopter. I'm sure Jeff was pondering his mortality when he called his loved ones in Canada to assure them that he was all right. It was one of the few times that I saw Jeff truly sad. He respected Stevie immensely, and I believe that Jeff felt like he'd lost a piece of his own life when his good friend died.

• •

Even at their height, musicians are always insecure. I knew I wasn't the world's greatest drummer. I was a blues drummer, and good at what I did. But I looked at Bon Jovi's drummer, Tico Torres, as one of the greats. So I was really touched when he complimented my drumming. He told me, "You're a hard hitter. I love a drummer who hits hard."

Jeff overheard the conversation and came over to investigate. "Well, I guess you're not so bad after all," he said with that little smirk.

I was really enjoying the tour at this point. When our band was on a roll, we could blow the biggest groups off the stage. I guess we had it right.

After we'd been with Bon Jovi for a few weeks, I was standing by the elevator when a stunning blonde grabbed me and pulled me in.

"Where are you going?" she asked.

"To my room."

"I'm coming."

"Okay. Why not?"

For the next two weeks, we became an item. She'd follow us from city to city and be at every show. Then, one night, she said something that made me realize that she wasn't getting it. She thought I was

Tico Torres is one of my idols, but do we really look that much alike?

Tico Torres, and never connected the dots. And it should have been easy to figure out. We'd actually *watched* Bon Jovi play together, and left before their final set was over. How she missed that is beyond me.

Of course, this became a good road story. Everybody had a good laugh. In fact, Tico came over to me before one show and said, "Hey, Tom, I hear you've been hanging out with my girlfriend."

Even on tour, Joe was always disciplined about practicing his martial art of choice, Muay Thai. He just managed to practice it at the wrong time. After some technical difficulties during a particular set, he went backstage, put on a training glove and began punching a concrete wall. "The wall won, and I broke two small bones in my hand," he said in our fan bulletin, *Jeff Healey Band Network*. "I misjudged the strength I had built up in my arms, and it was a foolish idea in the first place."

For the next six weeks, he performed in a small fiberglass cast, with a hole cut out for the thumb. This enabled him to hammer out his notes on the bass. Despite his condition, not one date had to be canceled. Still, "the pain of pulling through that, plus what I put Jeff and Tom through," he said, "taught me a much-needed lesson in self-control."

The truth is that Joe could be accident-prone. During a gig in London, we had an orchestra pit in the middle of the stage. The crew mapped it off with fluorescent tape so no one would fall in. Well, Joe had this crazy routine that involved doing all these martial arts kicks while he was playing. So he went into his act and, suddenly, we heard a crash. The next thing we saw was Joe's fingers trying to claw back up to the stage. At first, some of the crew was worried that Jeff — the blind guy — was the one who'd fallen. But, of course, it wasn't Jeff.

The guys on the crew didn't even attempt to disguise their laughter. Joe could be a pretty demanding guy on the road. For example, he had very strict requirements about where he wanted his Crown Royal placed onstage. If it wasn't exactly his way, he'd throw a fit. So as long as he could get up and continue the show, Joe didn't evoke that much sympathy.

On tour, the adventures kept coming. Dawna Zeeman, the general manager of Forte, remembers receiving a package one day from the Finnish police. "It was like 20 photos of a hotel room that seemed to be covered with blood and human organs and stuff. And the room didn't even belong to one of the Jeff Healey Band guys. It was one of our sidemen. The cops were doing some kind of investigation, so I wrote back, 'Oh, I heard about that. He had food poisoning and was violently vomiting.' I actually have no idea what happened. I didn't ask.

"There was another time when Jeff came home for Christmas. He had these videos of the band traveling and playing and hanging out. Everyone was sitting together and enjoying themselves. But Jeff didn't realize what they were watching because he was blind. Suddenly, Jeff's family got very quiet. And that's when Jeff realized the video was of Tom, fucking some girl."

One of our better gigs.

• •

After a show in Copenhagen, we ended up in a Hells Angels club-house. The guy behind the bar was a "striker," a cadet, basically, trying out for the club. Strikers are essentially slaves to the established members, and willing to do some crazy things to earn their colors. This particular guy's strategy seemed to be fucking with a rock drummer. There were no physical challenges — fortunately, since the guy would have destroyed me in a fight. But he kept doing dumb shit and asking me to match it. At one point, he bit the top of his beer bottle off and dared me to do something similar. Not to be outdone, I chewed off the top of my glass. Blood was spurting every-where — all of it mine.

"One of Tom's party tricks was chewing on a wineglass," recalls our guitar tech, Keith Rudyk. "There wasn't really a safe way to do this; there was sometimes a bit of blood, to be sure. It was like dealing with Keith Moon, except he was the guy who had to get up and steer the ship. Wherever we were going, Tommy always got us there and he got us out of there. Nobody ever died on his watch."

The next day, three of the biggest bikers I'd ever seen came backstage. We generally barred anyone from doing this before a show, but security seemed too timid to stop them. Everyone was intimidated until the bikers stopped and motioned at me.

"How is our little drummer?" one asked in a Danish accent. "You are a really crazy little fella."

We all had a good laugh, and the tension broke. The bikers ended up watching the whole show and loving it. As a consequence, they hired us to play a biker convention in France.

The weird thing about being a band is that you trip into these situations — both literally and figuratively.

We were escorted into the event by a motorcade of some 50 Harleys. As a motorcycle guy myself, I could have stood there the entire day, just gaping at the choppers. The opening act was a bunch of strippers — just like the days when we were starting out in Canada. Only now, we were receiving one of our best paydays ever.

These bikers were from all over the world, and a number of gangs. Yet, I don't remember feeling any friction or seeing any fights. We just met a lot of great people who loved our music and wanted to have a good time.

During a tour of Spain, we learned that B.B. King was opening for us. As a band, we were embarrassed. This was B.B., a gentleman we not only idolized, but the person who'd given us one of our biggest breaks. But he told us not to feel guilty. He liked playing in the early slot so he could go back to his hotel and get some sleep.

While in Spain, we played a few shows in bull rings. Onstage, Jeff would scream, "*Toro, toro, toro,*" like he was taunting a charging bull. We thought this was hysterical; when Jeff would stop laughing, I'd start. It was one of those jokes that got old because the audience didn't think it was all that funny. After about a week — with the

On my custom-made chopper back in Halifax.

crowd sick of hearing the bullfighting reference — we moved on to other things.

One night, a Spanish promoter took us up to a beautiful Greek restaurant, high in the mountains, overlooking the Mediterranean. Inside, there was a harpist, pianist and other traditional musicians playing, and Jeff wanted to jam. It was incredible to see these classical musicians in awe of this crazy, blind guy, the guitar spread out over his legs, playing a bluesy version of Spanish and Greek melodies.

Since there wasn't a drum set, I played on the table.

"*Opa!*" people yelled, smashing plates on the floor.

This is great, I thought. *I can smash things and it's all legal.*

"Opa! Opa! Opa!"

At some point, a donkey strolled through the restaurant, but no one paid it any mind — as if it were another customer. But I never forgot the sound of the amazing notes that Jeff played that night. He could perform any style, any time with anybody. It's one of the most treasured memories I have of hearing Jeff play.

• •

When the Rolling Stones came to Toronto for their *Voodoo Lounge* tour in 1994, we were invited to open for them at a secret event for rock 'n' roll insiders. My goal here was to get the Jeff Healey Band to open for the Stones on the road. I even had the perfect story line to feed to the press.

Back in 1977, Richards had been busted at the Harbour Castle Hotel in Toronto with 22 grams of heroin. When he went on trial the next year, one of his fans — a girl Keith called his "blind angel" — literally visited the judge's home and gave some one-on-one testimony about Richards's kind heart. She explained that Keith was so fond of her — and worried that she might be trampled because of her disability — that he made special arrangements for her to be escorted to a safe place whenever she appeared at a Stones show in Canada. Ultimately, the judge showed compassion. In lieu of prison, Richards was required to go into rehab and perform a benefit concert for the Canadian National Institute for the Blind.

Now one of the kids who'd benefitted from that organization, Jeff Healey, was grown up and ready to tour with the Stones as their opening act.

I don't know how Jeff felt about it, but it seemed like a pretty good strategy to me.

The first step, of course, was putting on a great performance in front of the Stones. That was the easiest part. With the hometown crowd going wild for Jeff, we blew everyone away. At one point, as I was playing, I looked over to the side and saw a little guy jammed between the speakers, shaking his head to the music. When I realized it was Mick Jagger, I nearly dropped my drumsticks.

After our set, we came back to our dressing room, where Charlie Watts and Ron Wood were hanging out. Ron had taken an interest in Jeff, so my plan seemed to be working. I was even more exuberant when Jeff was invited onstage with the Stones for their encore, accompanying them on the Al Green tune, "Can't Get Next to You."

After the show, Jeff, I and our tour manager at the time, Ben Richardson, ended up in an exclusive area backstage, just hanging with the Stones. Jeff was having a great time, mellowed by copious amounts of vodka and orange juice. Wood was extolling the virtues of Guinness, pressing Jeff to have some of his private stash.

Ben remembers, "As Jeff got more and more drunk, he became

*Jeff with Stones drummer Charlie Watts and backup singer Bernard Fowler
— before attempting to "teach" Keith Richards how to play guitar.*

happier and happier. I was standing, talking to Charlie Watts, right outside Keith's private dressing room. Then, Charlie led Jeff, past this behemoth of a security guard, inside. Charlie was snorting, as Keith stood there, changing his clothes with his pants around his knees. 'Hey, Keith, look,' Charlie smirked. 'It's Jeff!'

"Jeff drunkenly blundered into the room, grabbed Keith in a bear hug, and said 'Come on, Keith. We're going to go jamming at Grossmans and I'll show you how to play some real guitar.'

"Keith, just stood there, scowling, enveloped in Jeff's embrace, with his pants at his knees while the big security guy howled, 'No Charlie!' I stepped into the room and grabbed Jeff by the elbow. 'Come on, Jeff. Keith is changing. We should give him some privacy.'

"Tom was standing outside, furious. 'Jesus Christ Jeff,' he said, 'What the fuck were you doing? We got to get on this tour.'

"'Yeah, whatever, Tom,' Jeff said, turning to me. 'Ben, can you get the car? I got shit to do.'"

Not only were we not going on tour with the Stones, we were disinvited from the after-party that night.

Instead of talking to Charlie Watts about his cymbal ride pattern, I went back to the room I'd rented at the Four Seasons and trashed it. When the head of the Stones' Canadian security detail busted in and tried to stop me, I shoved him away. He grabbed me hard around the midsection, and slammed me on the bed. Then, he went over to the refrigerator, popped open a beer and handed it to me.

"By now, Tom, you should know that rock stars can be assholes," he said.

• •

When we were invited to open for ZZ Top, we were about as excited as we'd ever been. Billy Gibbons and the boys were just down-home good-time guys, and really impressed with Jeff and the band. Just like us, they'd started off as a blues group and transitioned into something bigger, so there was a lot we could learn from them. They were always around to provide knowledge or accommodate us in any way we wanted. At least at the beginning.

ZZ Top had a bus full of beautiful women that did nothing but follow them around. I'm not sure about their backgrounds: models and/or strippers, I assumed. Their sole job each night was to put on skimpy outfits, go out onstage, turn, bend down, show their butts to the audience and shake their boobs. As silly as this sounds, it was a crowd-pleasing routine, and probably worth the money it took to haul those girls to each town.

Jeff labeled their bus the "Chicken Coop." And as it turned out, we were the foxes.

As we traveled with ZZ Top from place to place, we began to sample the various girls. One night, I'd be with one. The next night, she'd be with Joe or Jeff, and I'd be with someone else. It seemed too

ZZ's girls instantly became fans.

good to be true and, like all things too good to be true, it came to a screeching halt.

The road manager for ZZ Top cornered me one day and started: "You're supposedly the manager?"

"Well, technically, we all manage . . ."

"I don't give a fuck who manages and who doesn't. Here's the situation. 'The Chicken Coop,' as I hear you boys call it — you end it right now, or you're off the tour."

Usually, I don't take well to be given an ultimatum. But I wasn't in the mood to argue. "Hey, we can get past the Chicken Coop," I said diplomatically. "No problem. The tour is too important to us."

When I told Jeff about the conversation, his attitude was a little less harmonious. "Fuck the road manager. Nobody owns those girls. They're free to do whatever they want to do . . ."

"You might be right. But the label is spending hundreds of thousands of dollars on us, and I really don't want to be put in a situation where I have to explain to them that we were kicked off the tour because of the fuckin' Chicken Coop."

For once, Jeff understood my logic. "Yeah, fuck it. I guess you're right."

To be honest, it's not like we were lacking for female company. So we adhered to our agreement, and the "little ol' band from Texas" treated Jeff like a pal. In fact, one day, Billy came over and invited us to go bowling.

"Bowling?"

"Yeah, bowling."

"Sure. Why not?" And off we went.

From a lifetime of practice, Jeff knew how to amaze people in this type of situation. Right off the bat, he knocked out a strike.

"You can't do that again," Billy challenged, and he was right. Jeff got a spare instead.

Billy scratched his beard and gave me a suspicious look. "You all just been jerking us around," he charged. "That boy can see. What kind of gimmick are you guys running?"

I had to tell Billy that I'd been hearing the same accusation since I joined the band. "Jeff's Jeff," I explained. "But trust me — he's blind as blind can be. Those aren't even his eyes."

"What do you mean, those aren't his eyes?"

"They're not real."

Prior to this moment, the guys in ZZ Top were impressed by Jeff's musicianship. Now they thought he was the coolest guy on the planet. After a few more drinks, when Jeff suggested he drive back to the hotel, Billy handed him the keys and slid into the passenger seat.

I was sitting in the back, playing a role that was all too familiar: "Jeff, left. No, no, no. Right. No. Left . . ."

I'd recently been at a celebrity golf tournament with Jeff when he'd insisted on driving the cart back to the main building. It was like being in the war, with things pinging off the vehicle from all

Jeff found a way to shock even ZZ Top.

directions. Unaware of where the pavement started, he just drove across the greens while golf balls were flying.

In this case, though, he did a really good job.

At around five that morning, I received a call from the front desk. "Sir, can you please come down here? We need your help with one of your associates."

"Which associate might that be?"

"Sir, just come now."

As I entered the lobby, no one spoke to me. The hotel staff simply looked over my shoulder and motioned. There was Jeff by the inside fountain, sound asleep and snoring in his underwear. I later found out that he'd gotten out of bed, mistaken the door to his room for the bathroom door, taken a very public leak, then decided that he needed to rest again.

Being a celebrity, he chose the most public place.

On a serious note, what ZZ Top taught us was invaluable. Those guys really knew how to run a band. I'll never forget sliding into business class on a plane when Billy walked past us with his guitar and a contingent of beautiful women — straight into economy class.

"How you all doing? Nice to see you boys wasting your money."

Lesson learned. It was one thing if we were flying across oceans. But for short hops, why *not* fly in economy class. In rock 'n' roll, pennies were often confused with dollars.

That said, whatever money Billy and his boys saved that night was blown when we played Las Vegas. Dusty Hill, the bassist and keyboardist for ZZ Top, was an avid gambler who enjoyed hitting the dice tables with a big cigar sticking out of his long beard. After a while, he let Jeff throw the dice for him — winning and losing large amounts at a time.

If that's how Dusty chose to spend his money, it was fine with me. The only thing I liked about casinos were the free drinks and meals. The way I saw it, I was already in the music business. That was enough gambling for one lifetime.

That said, I did indulge in a bit of gambling during our trip to the World Music Awards in Monte Carlo, where the bands with the best record sales were invited, with each band representing a specific country. In a weird way, it was like a rock 'n' roll Olympics, and a very big deal. In my drunken state, I accidentally won something in the area of $5,000. Not surprisingly, I didn't hold on to it very long.

By the time we arrived in Monte Carlo, we'd been on the road for about nine months. But we were excited to be part of such a grand event. Ringo Starr and Prince Albert were going to be hosting the awards ceremony, and being in that kind of company meant something to us.

Our road manager, Alan, was a lovely Scotsman who we called MacSound because he was also our soundman. Our journey with ZZ Top had taught us to have everybody working two jobs. Obviously, we paid them more, but we were trying to be economical. Generally, the parties ended up in MacSound's room, and when the band went out, he was always invited along.

MacSound was with Joe and I when we rolled into Flashman,

the hangout pub for the expats in Monte Carlo who were low-lifing it. It was similar to a neighborhood bar — only most of the people were millionaires. The three of us had grabbed a table when I heard Jeff calling my name. He was with Roy Lott, the number two executive after Clive at Arista — good guy, just straight as could be — dragging him through the open window of the pub to sit with us. Some of the best musicians in the world were in the place, sitting at the piano, singing any ditty they could remember between drinks. But when they saw Jeff, they stood up and gave him room. Everyone, it seemed, wanted to see him sit down at the keyboards and perform.

True to form, Jeff didn't disappoint. It was magical.

The party progressed from there — back to MacSound's room. And that's when things started to get out of hand. Someone literally hung off the chandelier and flew across the room. The thing exploded into bits and pieces.

MacSound was trying to call his wife in Scotland at the time, but got the answering machine. Here's the recording she preserved for posterity: "No, no. Please. Tom. Not that. *Smash!* Jeff, no."

At this point, our crew returned from hitting the pubs and informed me that there was a very important hockey game taking place in Canada, and if we positioned our television set a certain way, we could see it. We bent a couple of coat hangers and turned them into makeshift antennas, then I attempted to hang the television just outside the window — in the ninth floor of our atrium hotel. As I was attempting this feat, I looked at the balcony across from us and swore I spotted Ringo.

"Holy fuck!" I yelled to everybody in the room, "it's Ringo!"

There he was, wearing an ascot, with his hands in his smoking jacket, an impish grin on his face, taking in the scene. As the celebrants crowded around me at the window, I thought about shouting something witty to the former Beatle. But before I could, I dropped the TV set and watched it explode against the balcony.

Boom! That thing sounded like an atomic bomb. Everybody ran for cover. I decided to simply leave the room and extricate myself from the situation.

In front of the hotel, I ran into a couple of guys looking up at a series of poles flying the American, British and Canadian flags. Suddenly, they began pulling out money and arguing about which one could go up the flagpole and get his country's flag the quickest. Well, I had just been in Switzerland a few days earlier and had a brand-new army knife I'd purchased there. While the others were still debating, I shimmied up the pole and sliced off the Canadian flag.

When I returned to ground level, a gentleman in a white hat and white gloves was holding the back door of his vehicle open for me.

"What service," I said, stepping in.

"Sir," the man said in French, "you are under arrest."

Nobody searched me or confiscated my possessions when I arrived in lockup; since we were in Monaco, I guess it was an upper-class jail. Not long after I arrived, I noticed that the police were immersed in a poker game. Since I had a few thousand dollars in my pocket, I asked if I could play, too. Once they had soaked me of all my money, I was allowed to leave.

That was very fortunate for me. I was later told that, once you were arrested in Monaco, you were instantly exiled and banned from ever returning.

The night ended on the beach, where I fell asleep under a deck chair. I woke up in the morning with very clear marks from where the sun had burned through the slats. I looked like a fucked-up zebra.

At the hotel, I immediately ran into MacSound, who was pacing around in an agitated state. "Where the hell have you been, man? We have to practice for live."

We were the only band actually playing at the ceremony that night; everyone else was lip-synching.

Generally, I'd remember a detail like that. But MacSound had made a mistake and told us that we had the day off. He apologized for the confusion and shuttled me back to my room to take a quick shower. As I emerged, I felt too hungover to even imagine hitting a drum. I also realized that, somewhere in the course of the night, I'd broken some fingers. But Jeff was so tough on a day-to-day basis, and Joe had played for all those weeks in a cast. A small detail like broken fingers wasn't going to stop me. No matter what, the show had to go on.

When we stood in the reception line before the ceremony, the tan lines on my face were the only hint of what had occurred the previous night. But as we were being introduced to Ringo, he turned to Prince Albert and said, "Oh, Your Highness. This is the lad we've all been talking about. The drummer from the Jeff Healey Band." The Prince looked at me with a large grin. Ringo mumbled something that sounded like, "Well, Your Highness, drummers will be drummers."

That night, we kicked ass onstage, living up to the reputation that the Jeff Healey Band had worked hard to earn. Whether we were playing for an audience of bikers in Moose Jaw, Saskatchewan, or royalty in Monte Carlo, we always rocked the place. The show was magic, and the crew guys told me it was one of my best performances. Jeez, I guess I should have broken more fingers, gotten arrested and burned myself more often.

fifteen

There's an irony in the name of our 1992 album, *Feel This*, that I didn't recognize until now. For much of the time that we were in our studio — at Forte Records, in the modern mansion we'd converted in the Forest Hill section of Toronto — it didn't feel quite right. Again, the talent was there. It was an okay record, but we were a little bankrupt for ideas. At times, I really felt like we were stretching it.

After growing accustomed to seeing our videos played everywhere, and walking into places and immediately being treated better than the rest of the human population, at some point I realized, *God, there are a lot of assholes around, getting in our headspace and trying to control us.* The instinct under these circumstances is to rebel — against the record company, and against each other. In my normal life, if I had a friend who got on my nerves, I'd take a little break and get the agitation out of my system until I was up for hanging out with him again. But we couldn't do that as the Jeff Healey Band. We were making money together, and were pretty good at it. So we were stuck.

Not every band falls into this trap. Groups like Rush had a system that allowed them to tour for a few months before dispersing and allowing each member to do his individual thing. When they got back together, everything would feel fresh. In our case — and I largely blame myself for this — we'd get ourselves locked into these endless tours that would wear us down.

Yet there were those moments when everything seemed to work. Paul Shaffer, the fellow Canadian I'd tried so hard to find when we were hoping to score a record deal in New York, was now our peer, and ended up playing keyboards on *Feel This*. His memories of that era are different than mine. He remembers us as an "organic" unit: "The songs always came together quickly, in one or two takes. They were a live band, and were trying to capture that in the studio. So they didn't over-rehearse or play too many times."

While Jeff hated being compared to other blind front men like Ray Charles, Stevie Wonder and Ronnie Milsap, Shaffer saw a parallel: "What they have in common is they think music when they make music, no distractions, 100 percent concentration."

Another keyboardist we brought in was Washington Savage. I don't think we worked with many musicians at his level. He was as good at his craft as Jeff was at his. In the studio, he'd challenge, teach and excite Jeff. After a session with Washington, Jeff would tell me, "That's the real shit." He *never* talked about other musicians like that.

I know this sounds immature — because it was — but I was jealous of Washington. All of a sudden, he was Jeff's new friend. And he had it all. Like Jeff, he was a great musician and music historian. And he was handsome, always in leather with spiked hair and granny glasses. A lot of you are too young to get this reference, but he was cooler than Linc from *The Mod Squad*. He was a woman slayer, too. When we all hung out together, we took *his* leftovers. And it was *our* band.

But there was one time when I wasn't envious of Washington.

Left to right: Mischke, Tico Torres, Washington Savage and Jeff.

We were doing a television appearance in Germany. He'd never sung backgrounds before and seemed confused when a microphone was placed in front of him. As we performed, he put his lips to the mic, then began flailing on the floor. We all thought that he'd had too much to drink on the plane. But he was straight-out electrocuted.

• •

Joe had recruited engineer Rich Chycki to work on the record; not only did he oversee the studio, he played dobro on *Feel This*, as well. "The band was riding quite a wave," he says. "Their first album and *Road House* were very successful. Everybody considered *Hell to Pay* a really good album. So the vibe was very rock star, with demos coming in all the time from people looking to get their songs covered by Jeff. And sometimes they got through. 'Lost In Your Eyes' was one of the more popular songs on *Feel This*, and that was a submitted song. Tom was always about finding the single that would turn into a hit."

Rich was usually there when we arrived at the studio for a session, making sure that tape was rolling to capture whatever we came up with. "We were just going through miles and miles of multi-track tape — or, at the very minimum, DATs (digital audio tape) — to record everything. They'd sit and work on something, and it would turn into this long jam. At the end of the day, I'd give Tom a bunch of cassettes, and they'd disappear into the vortex unless the band thought there were any bits they could use."

At times, Jeff would take a walk around the house as he contemplated which sections worked. "He'd move as confidently as someone who had vision," Rich said. "He had everything calculated in that house, distance-wise, in terms of where he stepped. But the house rule was, 'Don't put shit in the way.' There were times when someone would leave a door halfway open, and Jeff would ding himself on the edge. It wasn't a funny thing, but he was nonchalant about it, the way he could be about everything. Sometimes we'd be talking and he'd ask me if I saw something on TV. And then, later on, I'd think, 'Hey, a blind guy was asking me if I saw shit.'"

Because of the nature of his job, Rich would often isolate himself in the studio while other things were happening in the house. "All of the sudden, I'd open the door, and there's 75 people hanging out, with catering going on. Tom would be surrounded by 10 girls, listening to pieces of the new record. And he'd hand me a beer and say, 'Here, play us some songs.'

"I might show up on a Sunday morning and walk into a party that was still going on from Saturday night, with four or five girls in various states of nudity hanging out in the hot tub. Or I'd be working late at night, and some girl would walk in, ask for Tom, then go upstairs. And I'd just shake my head and go back to work. That was a nice perk of the job. The scenery was great."

One night, I was with my friend, Mark Holmes, from the band Platinum Blonde, when I heard there was a party going on at the

Healey manor. Of course, I was the last person to find out about it. Mark had a friend who offered to give two ladies and I a lift in his vintage sports car. I should have been suspicious when I saw him snap back a few shots of tequila. But I was drinking, too, so didn't take it too seriously. The driver was doing 60 m.p.h. in a 30 m.p.h. zone, coming up to a stop sign and not slowing down. I grabbed the wheel, as we were about to crash into the front of a restaurant. We screeched across an intersection into a gas station and collided with one of the pumps.

With blinding smoke everywhere, I heard the driver ask, "What did I do to my car?"

"Fuck the car!" I yelled. "We have to get out of here before the whole thing blows up!"

One girl panicked, and couldn't release her seat belt. I pried it loose and shoved her toward the door. But it was stuck and wouldn't open until I kicked it a few times. Suddenly, Mark Holmes appeared with a giant friend we called "Big Steve." As Steve used his big hands and strength to reach down and pull us out, the flames erupted, creating a funnel on each side of us. Mark and Big Steve rushed the group to safety, while I ran off in the opposite direction to pull a fire alarm. Still, I knew that the police were on the way and didn't want to stick around. So I hopped a fence, ripping my suede pants on a sharp piece of mesh. I couldn't decide what I was angrier about — the accident or tearing my new pants.

I made it back to the house, and changed. The girls were already there, and pretty shaken up. I just continued partying.

The next day, my girlfriend at the time called. She'd driven by the ruins of the gas station and the car, and her sixth sense just told her that I'd somehow been involved. She was extremely upset. "If you keep going like this," she warned, "you're not going to last."

I actually took her words seriously, and vowed to slow up my partying. *Maybe the whole thing is getting out of control,* I thought. It was a resolution that only lasted until the next crazy tour.

At our party, just after the gas station blew up.
The next day, I decided to cut back drinking for a while.

"Everyone in the band played his role," Rich Chycki says. "Of course, Jeff was the focus on the band, and Joe was the background of the rhythm section. Tom was the manager and the drummer, playing both sides of the fence, which was an incredibly difficult position to maintain. Since then, I've met other people in the industry who wear multiple hats because they want their band to succeed, but Tom was the first one I knew. I always had the feeling that he took the job — at least at the beginning — because nobody else wanted it. So there'd be these situations where he'd be on the phone, doing management stuff, getting all worked up and yelling, and then he'd have to put down the phone, go back into the studio and play the drums."

Mischke, who'd been with us on the *Hell to Pay* tour, was one of our backup singers on the album — which was a pretty big honor for us, now that I think about it, since he's worked with performers like Jennifer Lopez and Michael Jackson. Jeff loved Mischke because his grandmother owned a record store in Detroit, and he could talk about Cannonball Adderley and other great jazz musicians who'd passed through there. For a period, the two lived in the same building, and Mischke began converting some of Jeff's old 78s to DAT tape.

"Sometimes he'd call me to come down," Mischke says, "and he'd ask for a certain record. I'd find it and put it on his player and start recording it, and then we'd talk about how amazing this particular artist was."

One of the benefits of recording at Forte was that Jeff was in his familiar environment, where he could listen to his records whenever he wanted, walk around Toronto and stop into a restaurant he liked and order a hamburger. Bret Gallagher, the future southern California president of Live Nation, remembers walking down Queen Street in Toronto and instantly recognizing Jeff's guitar sound coming out of some club that he'd wandered into to jam.

"There'd be nights when Jeff would drive up to the studio in a cab and he'd lay down the most incredible solo with the meter running," says Keith Rudyk. "And he'd yawn. He wouldn't even want to hear a playback. He'd rip a song apart, grab his cane and off he'd go."

Because Jeff was recording on his home turf, I think he developed a fondness for *Feel This* that lingered long after the album was released. "The scary thing is that I still like the record," he told an interviewer after the album came out. "I mean, with the other albums that we did . . . by the time we were finished making them, I would never want to hear from them again."

Despite his contention later on that he never really liked rock 'n' roll, Jeff sounded very different in an interview with our fan bulletin: "The album proves just how hellbent the band is on making rock 'n' roll that's honest and unique, with the amp up just enough to give you a jolt." In fact, it was Jeff who emphasized that the same album would sell 40 percent less in the blues section of the record store than in the rock section — a point I'd never argue, since no one knew more about records than Jeff.

Feel This included a really good tune by Tom Petty, "Lost In Your Eyes." Unfortunately, one of the best original songs to come out of the sessions was never released. "Bish, Bam, Boof" was an incredible instrumental with Jeff playing full-on fusiony distortion jazz. This was free-form, the way that we performed onstage, and we were lucky that the tape was rolling when Jeff was going crazy. Unfortunately, we were under pressure to produce hits, and this didn't fit the criteria at the time. In retrospect, I should have pushed back and demanded that the song go on the album. I'm confident that it will be released at some point, and — with the hindsight of the passage of time — recognized for the jewel that it is.

In 1992, though, my mind was on other battles. With the radio landscape changing so drastically, we made the decision to put a rapper named Jr. John on our track "If You Can't Feel Anything Else." It was a bizarre song, with Jeff playing almost country and these chicks singing in the background — not necessarily a bad track, but strange. Given all the shifts in the industry, I guess I thought we were being contemporary.

Obviously, a lot of people didn't agree with our choices. *Feel This* sold one hundred thousand records, a pretty big letdown from our previous work. The critics were brutal, calling our music clichéd corporate rock.

What was funny about this was that, a few years earlier, the same reviewers were praising us as the saviors of music. Now I was reading that Joe and I were horrible and Jeff was running out of gimmicks. Same fuckin' band! In fact, with all those hundreds of shows we had behind us, we were a far better band. When you do so much touring, you don't get worse, you improve. Sometimes, I knew what Jeff was doing before he did it. That's how tight we were as a band.

The problem is that when you hear and read this kind of stuff — even if you *say* it's all bullshit — somewhere deep inside, it has an impact. Then add cocaine into the mix during those late-night parties where tongues are wagging, and you wake with both a hangover and all that treacherous blathering from the night before stuck in your brain. Artists in general are insecure and don't take criticism well. Jeff's wry humor could make anyone paranoid. And it didn't help to have friends and associates going to each member of the band individually and repeating gossip allegedly gleaned from "reliable" sources.

As much as the three of us could all be jackasses, the ones outside the band were far worse.

"They went through a fair amount of tour managers," Mischke says. "I remember one of them seemed particularly shady. And one night, after about five shows, the guy claimed that he'd been robbed of like $25,000 in cash. He even stabbed himself in his hotel room and rushed himself to the hospital to make the whole thing look real. Everyone had to take him at his word; there weren't any security cameras. But we all knew who stole the money."

But for every one of these calamities, there'd be 10 other experiences that reminded me of how grateful I was to be in the music business. One night in Toronto, Bryan Adams's agent, Carl Leighton-Pope, invited me to a little restaurant in Chinatown on the proviso that, when I got there, I do a lot of listening and very little talking. When I arrived, I understood why. Seated at the table was all six foot five of Peter Grant, the legendary manager of Led Zeppelin. An imposing figure in his day, Peter had lost some weight and now walked with the aid of a cane. But he could still tell a story, and for the next few hours I listened like I was in a PhD class.

At one point I asked him why Zeppelin had rarely played Canada. Grant explained that his security team — who were notorious brutes — had been instructed to neutralize any bootleggers they found at a concert. In Vancouver, they spotted a guy holding up a device with a flashing red light. Convinced they'd detected a taper, they pulled him out of the crowd and hurled him down a staircase. "As it turns out," Peter continued with a slight smirk, "he was some sort of government official who was there to test the decibel level. When the concert was over, we had to dash for the Starship (the Boeing 720 that Zeppelin used as its official plane), and we never really played much in Canada after that."

Damn! Now, that's a story!

Whatever you think of Grant and his tactics, it felt pretty cool to be able to go to the source with a question I'd long pondered.

But there were a lot of cool moments.

When the Canadian embassy in Washington, DC, held a birthday party for bluesman Ronnie Hawkins, the three of us were invited. As we were leaving, we were stopped by these Secret Service agents who checked our IDs and asked if we had ties.

"Ties?" I asked incredulously. "We're in a rock band, man, leaving a party. Why the hell would we have ties?"

"Well, can you get some ties?"

"Nope."

"What about jackets?"

I realized the guy was just doing his job. "No, sir. But if we're *leaving* the embassy, why do you care if we have ties and jackets?"

Suddenly, I spotted Ronnie and his wife. "What's going on?" I asked him.

There was a car at the curb, and he instructed us to get in. "You'll figure it out."

The moment we turned onto Pennsylvania Avenue, I remembered our conversation with Bill Clinton back when he was governor of Arkansas. He'd talked about his admiration for Ronnie Hawkins, and promised, "One day, you boys can come visit me at the White House."

Even Clinton's political enemies conceded that he was a genius, a guy who never forgot a face or a conversation. Say what you want about politicians; when Bill Clinton promised *us* something, he proved to be a man of his word.

Some White House handler was there to remind us to keep our expectations low: "Only speak when spoken to. Let the president do the talking. You'll probably be with him for about five minutes, and with a little luck, the president likes you all and you'll get a picture."

Jeff wasn't having any of it. The moment that we were led into the Oval Office, he blurted, "Hey, I remember you. Aren't you the governor? I see you've moved up in the world."

Clinton seemed to have a good laugh over that.

Ronnie then proceeded to tell one of the most off-color jokes I'd ever heard — and I've heard a lot of them. Apparently, so had Clinton. "Not bad, Ronnie," he responded. "But did you ever hear this one?"

Clinton's joke was dirtier — although I don't think that would surprise anyone.

Jeff and the president launched into a conversation about old records, blues, jazz and their shared love of Louis Armstrong and Jelly Roll Morton. It was magical and fantastic.

Our 5 minutes turned into 45. That's when Clinton turned away from Jeff and asked me, "Where did you say you're from?"

"Sorry, Mr. President. We're all based in Toronto. None of us will be able to vote for you."

"Well," Clinton replied with grinning finality, "I guess that takes care of that. See you all later."

With those words, we were all ushered out the door. But I couldn't help feeling taken in by Bill Clinton's charisma. He made you feel special, and really understood music. There was a warmth he exuded that helped me understand why so many African-Americans grew to refer to him as "our first Black president" and his love of Ronnie led to this wonderful experience.

As you can imagine, there were even more guidelines when we were invited to a meeting with Queen Elizabeth II during Canada's 125th anniversary celebrations, along with fellow Canadian artists Gordon Lightfoot, Robbie Robertson, Neil Young and David Foster. There was a long reception line, and Jeff was feeling a little bored. So we were joking around, just to kill time, when a protocol officer demanded that we stop talking.

As rock 'n' rollers, we weren't used to being addressed this way. "What is this, school?" I challenged.

"No talking," he emphasized.

When it was finally our turn to meet the monarch, she stood in

*Proud Canadians meeting the queen. David Foster and
Gordon Lightfoot can be seen in the background.*

front of Jeff with her hand extended. But because she hadn't addressed
him, Jeff didn't know she was there. I didn't want the queen to look
stupid, so I quietly explained to her, "I'm sorry, Your Majesty. This is
Jeff Healey."

Now she realized that Jeff was blind. The queen looked at Joe
and me and gave us cursory nods. Then, she reached out, took Jeff
by the hand and said, "Hello, Jeff. It's just me. *The queen.*"

After she moved on, the protocol officer came back, apoplectic.
"You know you're never supposed to talk to the queen unless she
talks to you first," he shouted.

"You know what?" I yelled. "Go fuck yourself. If you don't have
enough sense not to embarrass the queen by telling her that she was
meeting someone who's blind, then fuck you."

Fortunately, the queen never heard my temper tantrum. Really,
the guy was an asshole.

On the other hand, who knew the queen was so cool?

sixteen

I guess this is as good a place as any to mention that, with all the other craziness that was going on, Jeff got married in 1992. His wife, Krista Miller, exuded positive energy and shared a lot of Jeff's interests. Her father was a record collector and probably had thousands of 78s in his home, the way Jeff did. In fact, that's how Jeff met Krista, through her father.

When someone else finds domestic bliss, we're supposed to be happy for them. But — through no fault of Krista's — marriage drove yet another wedge through the band. Why would Jeff want to be with us when he could go home, talk about music with his wife — the two later had a daughter together — and play his trumpet in solitude? Well, the truth is he *didn't* want to be with us as much anymore. In some ways, the band became like school or a nine-to-five job — an obligation. There might be moments during the day when you have a few laughs, but the whole time you're thinking about the better things you'd rather be doing.

I could feel Jeff pulling away and — I'm not going to lie about this — sometimes I pouted and acted like a jealous boyfriend. My critics would say I was clinging to Jeff because he was my meal ticket. But they weren't around when we were driving to gigs in the frozen tundra, talking and laughing and sharing the same dreams. Now that fame and adulthood had hit, I missed my old friend.

Yet I didn't always express that emotion in the most constructive way.

"Tom could get into really bad moods," remembers Mischke. "It was a very drinking band, so there was going to be tension, from alcohol and being stuck in such close quarters all the time. I remember getting into it with him in the alleyway between the Roxy and the Rainbow on Sunset Strip. The band was in a limo that was a little wider than most. Tom kicked the door open. And when he did, a car came along and smashed it. According to what the limo driver said, the door came clear off the car, and he had to get out, pick it up and put it in the trunk.

"So now Tom had to go into crisis-management mode. He wanted Jeff and all of us to get out of there right away and go back to the hotel. I was having a good time and didn't feel like going anywhere. And when I told him this, he started yelling at me.

"Between being in the studio and touring, I'd been with these guys for a close to a year, and I wasn't in the mood for Tom to tell me where I was going and what I was supposed to do. And he kept on and on, and at some point, he started coming at me.

"Now, Tom's a pretty strong guy. Back in those days, you didn't want to have anybody but that guy by your side in a fight. And I think Jeff knew instinctively, from the sound of Tom's voice, that I'd pushed him too far. So he got between us. And Jeff was pretty big. When Tom gets angry, he's kind of unstoppable. But Jeff was holding him back and telling me to shut the fuck up. He finally lets go of Tom and pulls me aside and says, 'It is what it is, man. We're leaving.'

"The irony, of course, is you could never tell Tom to leave a club if he was having a good time. If he wanted to stay, you couldn't say no to him. If you told him to leave, you'd be committing a cardinal sin."

We were finally home after touring nonstop when, out of nowhere, these rich Canadians called me about flying the whole band down to the Cayman Islands for a Canada Day gig. We were just too tired, I answered. Maybe next year. But these Canadians were really insistent. The money was great and they said that we could come early, make it a vacation and stay as long as we wanted. When I ran this by Jeff, surprisingly, he decided that he wanted to go.

The crew flew down a couple of days before us. When the band got off the plane, the road manager met me at the bottom of the stairs, handed me a brown paper bag with a straw sticking out and said, "Drink up." But he didn't hand anything to Jeff or Joe.

On the way to the hotel, I found out why. There was some Aussie who considered himself the drinking champ of the island. For the last two days, he'd been challenging our guys to drinking contests and killing them. After one competition, a member of our crew jumped into the sea all drunk, threw up and was attacked by fish. So now, in advance of Canada Day, my fellow Canadians wanted me to start training to restore the honor of our country.

Jeff got really into it. "If anyone can beat this fuck, you can," he said. "Tom, we need you to do this." Everybody was caught up in it. Even the locals were making bets.

With two days to go before the show, I was taken to meet the Aussie. The guy was a monster, and he kind of smirked like, "This is the little bloke who's going to beat me?"

We agreed to the rules: the first one to fall down loses. Then we flipped a coin to see who would choose the alcohol. The Aussie won and picked vodka — not a drink I generally do well with.

For the entire day, we sat across from each other, draining one drink after another. By nighttime, we were wobbly, but both able to stand.

As I staggered back to my seat, Jeff came up behind me and whispered, "If we switch to rum tomorrow, we might get him."

I looked across at the Aussie and proclaimed, "At 12 — rum."

He shook his head. "We can't do this forever, mate. Why don't we make a gentleman's agreement to start again in the morning?"

I could sense fear and weakness. "No way," I shot back. "We keep going."

By 5 a.m., the tournament had relocated to some rich guy's house. I don't remember if the owners were Australian or Canadian, but everyone was having a great time, raising their bets and watching the two of us practically kill ourselves, like two roosters in a cockfight.

I was pretty fucked up, but I could tell my opponent was on his last legs. So I decided to challenge him to shots of tequila. His face was red and sweaty, and I could see that he wasn't so sure. There wasn't any way he could say no, though, with his boys egging him on: "Come on, you can take this little wanker."

So we went. Shot. Shot. Shot. And finally, the Aussie puked and collapsed on the kitchen floor.

At that instant, somebody threw a coconut into the kitchen. One of the Aussies picked it up, put his head down and started to run across the room like it was a rugby game. On instinct, I tackled him. When the coconut slipped out of his hands, the drinking champ — who I thought was finished for the night — got a second wind, jumping up, grabbing the coconut and crashing into everything. In the commotion, somebody fell through a glass door. Dishes and glasses were being smashed. I mean, we destroyed that kitchen.

At that moment, I had a flashback to my youth. My mother finally left my father after *he* had a drunken rugby game in *our* house and the refrigerator got knocked over.

Fortunately, this wasn't my mother's house.

I had a day to sleep it off before our show. When we finally hit

187

the stage, we got through four songs before the skies opened up and rain started pelting the band and the audience.

"Talk about a gig that goes sideways," says our guitar tech, Keith Rudyk. "Things were floating across the stage, pedal boards and shit."

When a flash of lightning appeared over the ocean, the organizers, scared that Jeff was going to be electrocuted, called off the concert. Before they did, I hit the bass drum and heard something crack in my foot. Apparently, I'd injured myself during the rugby game, and now had to go back to Canada in a wheelchair. So I guess that Australian jackass got his revenge on me.

• •

In 1995, we did an album completely devoted to other people's songs, *Cover to Cover*. When you do a cover album, it means you're creatively destitute. The band was no longer writing original material; Jeff wasn't feeling motivated. On top of that, he was bugging me to get us off the label. Now, Clive and the other people at Arista had been pretty good to us. We needed a breather, and they let us do an album of cover material. But Jeff told me he'd had enough of the record business.

Some bands do whatever the fuck they want to do and deal with the consequences. I seriously doubt that a group like AC/DC ever paid attention to the trends. Maybe we should have done a blues record and taken our chances. If it sold nine million records, we'd be bigger than ever. And if it sold one thousand records, at least we'd know we had a good album. But, in Jeff's mind, we'd become beholden to our masters, and he hated it.

From a record company's point of view, "the easiest part of interacting with a band is when they are on their way up," says Tom Ennis, Arista's product manager for the Jeff Healey Band. "When sales start to decline, that's when things become a little bit harder. There were times when Tom would ask for something, and I knew it wasn't coming from him, but from Jeff. He probably should have been either a manager or a drummer. Trying to play both roles is almost impossible."

While we were preparing for *Cover to Cover*, we put on a show at Grossman's Tavern to test-run our material at the place where we started, and see how the crowd would respond. It felt like the old days. Rob Light, who'd end up heading the Creative Artists Agency's music division — and working with acts like AC/DC, Fleetwood Mac, Katy Perry and James Taylor — remembers the feeling of walking into a joint and realizing that he was witnessing a Jeff Healey performance. "I have always been a guitar freak," he said. "The magic of watching the greats effortlessly turn a piece of wood and six strings into pure energy and emotion always got me going. The first time I saw Jeff play a guitar on his lap, my jaw dropped. I have seen lap steel players, but never a world-class player create rock and blues the way that Jeff did. There was a ferocity to his playing that just took the audience to another level."

Recalls Ennis, "Playing live was the best thing for the band. Because the expectation was not putting out hit singles. It was getting on stage and kicking ass, which they could always do."

We had our crew to record everything from the truck outside. It was one of the best times we had during this period, but no one heard this music for 16 years — until *Live at Grossman's* was released as an album in 2011.

Despite everything else that was going on, all of us wanted a superstar producer who'd make the best out of whatever we recorded. Thom Panunzio was busy in L.A. and really didn't want to come up to Toronto and lock himself into our world at the Forte studio. He said that Jeff got him on the phone, and begged him to change his mind:

"He tells me, 'Look, I really need your help. And I don't want to record the album in Los Angeles. I'm not really comfortable away from home. It's really difficult for me. I'm scared of going other places. I don't know my way around. In Toronto, I can walk home from the studio. My mother is sick and I really want to be near her.

Can you please come and help me? We'll do it real quick.' When he spoke to me like that, from the heart, I couldn't say no."

Panunzio wasn't all that happy in Toronto. The gear wasn't up to his standards, and we had to import equipment from L.A. As Jeff's mother's health worsened, he began leaving sessions early to take care of her. And Arista wasn't exactly enamored with the songs we decided to cover.

Did the songs suck? Of course not. We did a killer version of Creedence Clearwater Revival's "Run Through the Jungle," and two excellent Jimi Hendrix songs, "Angel" and "Freedom." I think our renditions of "Yer Blues" by the Beatles, and Stealers Wheel's "Stuck in the Middle with You" are up there with the originals. Jeff was adamant about doing a Robert Johnson song but shied away from "Crossroads" and "Walkin' Blues" because they'd been covered so many times. After talking to a friend at the Robert Johnson Foundation, he decided on "Stop Breakin' Down," and everyone was happy with it.

All in all, we probably recorded 40 songs, and whittled the album down to the best 14.

Sometimes, when we were around outsiders, we'd been able to fake unity in the band. But Panunzio immediately saw that things were fracturing. I'd purchased the Forte mansion as a tax write-off that ended up saving the band more than a million dollars. But because I was living there, there was all this bitching from people associated with the group, and Thom heard every word of it: "Tom Stephen is living in the band's mansion, while Jeff has to walk home by himself in the cold."

No one bothered to mention that I'd chosen to live in the place that was the band's headquarters, and never had a moment away from the business. That's dedication, if you don't mind me saying so. But no one complained about it when I was living on a dirt floor and *that* was our office.

"While we were finishing up the album, Tom would come up to me and say, 'Jeff's becoming very difficult to deal with,'" Panunzio says. "And Jeff would say, 'You've got to be harder on Tom.' He was losing patience with the band because, let's face it, he was the outstanding musician in the group. Getting the right drum parts, keeping the time and all that, is always the hardest thing to do on a record. And then the bass has to be with it. So Jeff was getting very critical of his bandmates. He wanted this, they wanted that. And Arista kept changing their minds about the songs. Jeff was under enormous pressure because of his mother. And it was taking longer to make the record than anyone thought."

To make matters even more complicated, we'd been trying to branch out and manage other artists. On the eve of her 17th birthday, a beautiful singer named Amanda Marshall was at an autograph signing with her father. The two approached Jeff, mentioned that they were fans and asked about the best way to get into the industry. There was something about Amanda that seemed pure, and Jeff felt comfortable inviting her to jam with us at Grossman's the next night. Once again, her father brought her to the club. Jeff played acoustic and Amanda sang. Right away, we realized we had a star on our hands.

I remember that the band was waiting to perform on David Letterman's show, and all Jeff could talk about was Amanda. Could I figure out how to get her a deal? I didn't see how we could miss. Despite her age, she had a presence — she was racially mixed, with blue eyes and long, blonde hair that curled past her shoulders — and her voice would impress anybody. We used her vocals on *Cover to Cover* but knew that she deserved to be in the spotlight.

Getting her a contract was one of the easiest things I ever accomplished. Donnie Ienner from Sony Music loved her, signed her and everything started moving quickly from there. What could possibly go wrong?

In a word, everything.

Stylistically, she was great at covers, but her vocal style wavered between blues and rock 'n' roll. But that wasn't a problem for Ienner. He came up with a plan to brand her as a modern-day Janis Joplin with a grunge twist.

I thought it was a great idea. Amanda didn't. "They want me to be Janis Joplin," she said. "Well, I'm not Janis Joplin. I'm me."

Maybe the problem was asking an artist to imitate another artist. Ienner already had Mariah Carey and Celine Dion. If Amanda didn't want to go along with his concept, he didn't need her on the label, and dropped her.

At this point, Amanda became withdrawn. Instead of concentrating on her singing, she spent a lot of time at home, bummed out. It was as if her soul were shattered.

But I knew the kind of talent she had, and wasn't about to give up. We flew down to New York, where I arranged a showcase for the different A&R guys. For the first time in her life, Amanda put on a bad show.

"You know what's wrong?" Jeff observed. "She's not turned on by her own voice."

After discussing the matter, we decided to bring her back to Canada and have her open for us on tour. It was a good arrangement for everyone involved. Amanda was excited again. Her depression seemed to lift, and she shed the pounds she'd been putting on. In every city, she expanded her audience base.

It took a while for Amanda to find herself. For five years, we had her on salary, while Forte paid for studio recordings, her band to go on the road and other expenses. We spent hundreds of thousands of dollars, but hung in with her through good times and bad. At one point, Jeff wanted to drop her, but I convinced him otherwise. Eventually, Richard Zuckerman and Mike Roth signed her to Sony Canada. Her 1995 debut, *Amanda Marshall*, was certified as a diamond record, the equivalent of 10 million units in the U.S.

Brian Adams, who'd always treated Jeff with the utmost respect, came in and wrote two amazing songs for her next project. I was pretty satisfied, since Brian's manager, Bruce Allen, had told me that I couldn't be a musician and manage. "*It's like being shirts and skins at the same time.*" Well, here I was, breaking Amanda Marshall, while

One of Canada's greatest managers, Bruce Allen.

still playing drums with the Jeff Healey Band. And Bruce's artist was now writing songs for her!

Unfortunately, my feeling of vindication was short-lived. Amanda refused to put either track on her album. And, I'm telling you, those tracks were over the top. Shortly thereafter, Bruce Allen called. I won't repeat his exact words, but let's just say they reinforced his original opinion of me.

Meanwhile, Amanda was opening up for Tears for Fears and John Mellencamp in America and headlining in Europe. Like the Jeff Healey Band before her, she was the focus of a 90-minute live special on Canada's MuchMusic network. At one point, Elton John came on Rosie O'Donnell's show and named Amanda as the new artist he liked most.

The statement knocked her career into the stratosphere. Amanda was happy, and her parents were happy. Everything should have moved smoothly from there. She just needed Jeff to keep encouraging her. But when I asked him to call her one day, he refused. "She can phone me," he said.

That's when I recognized that Jeff viewed Amanda's success as a threat — even though she was his discovery. And Amanda was just as stubborn. Despite her age, she'd come to believe that Jeff should be the one calling her.

At that point, I knew I was fighting a battle I'd never win. The dream fell apart. Jeff and Amanda were no longer a team. They didn't speak again until years later, when they both decided that they hated me.

CHAPTER
seventeen ─────────

When *Cover to Cover* was finally released, Jeff would tell interviewers that the album was special to us because, being a bar band, we'd always played covers to hold the audience. That part was true, but it wasn't the reason we did *Cover to Cover*. The label knew that we weren't really there, and never got behind the record.

Like our earlier albums, released when grunge and rap were overtaking the industry, *Cover to Cover* had to compete with music that was pretty far from what we were doing. In 1995, the number one song was Coolio's "Gangsta's Paradise," followed by tracks like "Kiss from a Rose" by Seal, "On Bended Knee" by Boyz II Men and "Fantasy" by Mariah Carey. Even so, we had the top blues album of the year, and our version of "Shapes of Things" was nominated for a Grammy for Best Instrumental Performance.

Ultimately, we lost to "Jessica" by the Allman Brothers. Also nominated was "Every Now and Then" by Santana with Vernon Reid. I'd grown up as a fan of Santana, and it was incredibly cool to be interacting with them as equals. Carlos Santana was always one of my favorite guitar players, and it was fun listening to him and Jeff talk about licks and ideas. At Clive Davis's party — which was the party everyone wanted to attend on Grammy night — Carlos was bringing Jeff around, introducing him to people.

"Jeff, this is Alice Cooper."

"Pleased to meet you, Jeff."

"Alice fuckin' Cooper?" I whispered to Jeff. "Where's the boa constrictor and the makeup?" Jeff laughed. Even though he couldn't see Alice, Jeff could sense the guy's conservative vibe. By the way he was dressed, Alice looked like a banker. The macabre act was just that, an outrageous gimmick that was good for business. I should have understood this by now, but the experience was another eye-opener into how the industry worked.

Unfortunately, our relationship with Clive was coming to an end. After badgering from Jeff, I respectfully — and reluctantly — severed our ties to Arista. Why would I do something that stupid? Here's why. We were the *Jeff Healey* Band, and when Jeff Healey said he was finished with the record business, I took him at his word. Another manager would have fought him. I'd fought with Jeff enough. There was no sense pushing a guy who refused to be pushed. When all was said and done, we were friends, and I wanted him to be happy.

"Jeff could love you one day and hate you the next," says Stevie Salas. "I was onstage with him in London and he told me I sucked, I sounded like shit. That was how Jeff was. He'd talk like that to anybody. And no one ever said 'fuck you' to Jeff. And then, another time, in San Diego, Jeff told me I was amazing. So you never knew where you stood with Jeff.

"When we were in San Diego, we were playing at the Belly Up, a famous place in Solana Beach. I had a place on the water with a boat dock, and a group of us came back to my house to go waterskiing at two in the morning. The girls didn't have bathing suits, so they stripped down to their bras and panties. One of them was this really hot redhead with an hourglass figure, a DJ, and she and Tom disappeared into the bathroom. I got up on a box to look in the window and soon, everyone else was up there, standing next to me. We're all waiting for him to give it to her. But he just goes down on her for 45 minutes while she's sitting on the sink. We all got so bored, we left. But that's the way Tom was. He's going to please Jeff, and he's not going to stop until he pleases (this girl)."

A short time later, we were playing some gigs around the northeastern United States, and Jeff was acting like he was a slave who'd just been sprung from the plantation. All he kept talking about was the sweet taste of freedom. Then, one day in Boston, Jeff received a phone call and seemed to turn paler than he already was.

It seemed that Colin James had just signed a new record deal in Canada.

Jeff and Colin had been friends, and competitors, since their teens. Colin was raised as a Quaker in Regina, Saskatchewan, where he began writing songs, playing guitar and performing blues and rock.

You get the picture? Two guitarists — both Canadian and both blues guys.

Now, on the surface, Jeff and Colin were tight. On one of the few occasions when Jeff was too sick to make a gig, he asked Colin to fill in, and Colin came running. That's how much they respected each other. But when the press ran stories about the blues guitarist who was Canada's next big thing and gushed about Colin, Jeff would go nuts. Like all the greats, Jeff was competitive.

If memory serves me correctly, Colin's deal was just for Canada. Not America. Canada. But as soon as Jeff got off the phone, he was seething. We got into a limo to go to our gig, and Jeff was lost in his thoughts, not saying anything.

Finally, he spat out, "Colin James has a record deal and I don't. Where's my record deal, Tom?"

"Colin James has a record deal in Canada," I yelled back. "*Canada*, Jeff. That's it. Who the hell cares about this record deal in Canada? We just walked away from Clive Davis!"

"There was a lot of frustration in the band," remembers Ralph James, our agent during the later years of the group. "They thought they should have been bigger. And Tom could be a pain in the ass. Unreasonable. Whatever money we brought in was never enough. Jeff had learned a lot from Tom and wasn't naïve when it came to the financials. But what he really cared about was the artistic side. Tom just wanted to get the deal done so the band could get back to their music."

During this period, Stevie Salas told me that my biggest flaw was indulging Jeff. "Everything was about making Jeff happy," Stevie says today. "I loved Jeff. We were friends. But Jeff was making bad decisions, career-ending decisions, and Tom went along with them. Jeff's actions were destroying the brand, destroying the band. Tom let him get away with it. And Jeff couldn't see the light — no pun intended."

Fortunately for us, we had a lot of options. It seemed like it took minutes for us to sign with Atlantic Records founder Ahmet Ertegun. In reality, the process took a few weeks. But I had little to complain about. Going from Clive Davis to Ahmet Ertegun was hardly a step down. We were actually shifting from one giant to another.

Atlantic chairman and co-CEO Val Azzoli put the deal together. He was very attentive and persuaded us that Atlantic was a better fit for us than other labels. I know that Jeff liked that Val was a Torontonian. But Val also seemed to get where Jeff's head was at that time. He needed to get jazz out of his system, and Val was open to the possibility of releasing whatever jazz records Jeff wanted to make — as long as we also focused on creating a new Jeff Healey Band album.

It all seemed pretty reasonable to me. Yeah, I wasn't pleased about how we left Clive. But Jeff was doing things his way, and for a while he seemed happy.

Unfortunately, some deeply personal issues intervened, most

notably the death of Jeff's mother, Yvonne. I can't even describe the closeness that the two of them enjoyed. Jeff took great comfort in the fact that he'd been around while his mother was declining, caring for her the way she'd looked after him his entire life. Now he really seemed adrift without her.

"We had an acoustic guitar on the bus at all times," said our guitar tech, Keith Rudyk. "Jeff asked for it one night, and we were all kind of surprised. He didn't play recreationally on the bus anymore. But he wanted to play the songs his mother loved, country songs, George Jones, Johnny Cash, Eddy Arnold. It was intimate. Playing that music made him think of his mom.

"Joe and Tom were in the front of the bus, but they came back to listen. They played with Jeff every night, but they just stood there like the rest of us, captivated. It was a cherished moment. If I could go back in time and record any experience of my life, that would be it."

Jeff still had his dad, of course. But when Jeff heard that Bud Healey was dating again, it upset him. From what I know, Bud had done nothing but honor his wife while she was alive. He had a right to move on. Yet Jeff felt this enormous void and couldn't abide his father trying to close his own emotional gap.

It was around this time that Jeff decided to find his biological mother. Somehow, he thought that he could replace Yvonne and soothe the sense of loss. But the woman he tracked down was no Yvonne Healey. I felt that she was a bit of a hustler who thought she'd hit the jackpot by discovering that she had a famous kid. Suddenly, these low-life people were in Jeff's orbit, drinking in his celebrity and looking for handouts.

The whole thing was heartbreaking, and only served to distort Jeff's compass further.

To make matters worse, Jeff and his first wife, Krista, divorced in 1998. As embarrassing as this is to admit, the situation terrified me. The Jeff Healey Band was a business. If they'd had a bitter, protracted divorce battle, what hurt Jeff would have hurt all of us. But like Yvonne and Bud Healey, Krista was made from better fabric than the rest of mankind. You know what she wanted from Jeff? A home where she could raise their daughter and a college education. Instead of fighting over alimony, Jeff agreed to give Krista the house and pay her way through school. *That's it.* This enabled the two of them to continue to relate to each other as friends — which, of course, was great for their daughter.

She was a wonderful person. To this day, she continues to impress me.

More and more, Jeff's focus seemed to be outside the band. He'd been playing with a Toronto group called the Hot Five Jazzmakers for several years, specializing in classical jazz, particularly from the 1930s. The more he stayed off the road, the more energy he could devote to the Jazzmakers when they appeared at local clubs. Although he played guitar and lent vocals to the group's songs, he largely viewed himself as a trumpet player with this band.

"I don't class myself as a guitar player," he told *Guitar Player* magazine. "I'm a musician whose forte, or most prominent instrument is the guitar. But I dabble in lots of instruments and listen to lots of things, and I get ideas from all over the place. So, henceforth, I'm a musician."

What he didn't mention was when Les Paul heard Jeff play jazz in New York, the granddaddy of electric guitar quipped, "Jeff, you're the world's best guitar player, not the world's best trumpet player."

I understand why Jeff was enjoying the jazz band more than the Jeff Healey Band. No one was really demanding anything of him, so jazz became his refuge. He didn't have to confront questions like, "Is this record going to hit? Will this radio guy like my song? Is this tour coming through?"

When Jeff was either playing jazz or listening to his old records, he had peace of mind. I wish I'd realized this a little earlier, so we could have made the situation work better for Jeff and everybody else. By the time we were on Atlantic Records, we were financing some of Jeff's jazz projects. Forte Records and Productions also helped him with a Louis Armstrong retrospective he did for CBC and BBC Radio, built largely around Armstrong's outtakes, as well as those of bandleader and arranger Fletcher Henderson.

It was a really cool project, but I felt like a husband who was trying to recapture his wife's affection after years of misunderstandings that were never really discussed. So instead of giving a little bit to get a lot back, I was giving a lot and only getting a little back.

Yet, even under these circumstances, Jeff could liven up your life just based on who he was and how people reacted to him. One night, he was playing trumpet at a little joint when Tom Jones walked in. Jones had first distinguished himself in school as a trumpeter, and was mesmerized. They spoke between sets, and Tom couldn't believe the depth of Jeff's knowledge about the English jazz scene. When it was time for Jeff to play again, Tom joined him onstage.

Imagine what it must have been like to be a customer there that night — seeing Jeff Healey on trumpet and Tom Jones belting out his classic "Delilah." The scene reminds me of our first tour of England, when the cook on our crew would get hammered and sing "Delilah" with a wine cooler on his head, as we wailed along with him.

When the music ended, Tom gathered Jeff and all his friends and drank everyone under the table. Then, at 5 a.m., he rolled out of the place and went to the airport, no doubt to create more Tom Jones anecdotes for someone else in another city.

• •

In 1996, we were invited to play at the festivities surrounding the Summer Olympics in Atlanta — opening for none other than James Brown himself. "Hell, I want to do that," I told Jeff. If there were two things I loved, it was watching sports and listening to James Brown.

When we came offstage, Brown greeted us by saying, "Jeff, you're one motherfucking guitar player and your band's cool, too." *Wow, the godfather of soul said that?* I thought. *Unbelievable!*

After Brown left the room, some Scandinavian athletes came in and let me hold their gold medal. It was only when they mentioned that they'd earned it by defeating Canada that the mood was somewhat dampened.

But not for long. Onstage, James Brown burned the house down. The show was so loud, though, that none of us realized that, nearby in Centennial Park, a survivalist nut named Eric Rudolph had planted a 40-pound bomb loaded with nails and screws. The explosion killed one person and injured 111 others. Suddenly, I was being pushed outside, where the stench of gunpowder filled the air. There was screaming and ambulances and the flashing lights of other emergency service vehicles. And no sign of Jeff or Joe.

What had been one of the best nights of my life turned into a panic-stricken search for my buddies. I went back to the hotel, calling around to the police and hospitals. Without the aid of the internet, I wasn't sure who'd been hurt or killed.

When Jeff and Joe finally turned up, Jeff and I got into a really big fight. I was pissed that they'd gone out partying without bothering to tell me that they were okay.

"It's not a big deal," Jeff said.

To a degree, he had the right attitude. Even after the bombing — and dozens of copycat threats — the Olympics continued, and the crowds in Atlanta seemed to get larger. The city's mayor Andrew Young and Representative John Lewis — one of my personal heroes — later compared Atlanta's defiance and determination to the civil rights struggles of the 1960s.

CHAPTER
eighteen ———————————

Eventually, Jeff opened Healey's, a cool little jazz club on Bathurst Street in Toronto. The club allowed him to indulge his musical passions and highlight Canadian acts, giving back to the city that gave him so much. Plus his fans in Toronto could see him play practically on a weekly basis, an opportunity they never forgot. Jeff's involvement with Healey's also provided him with an excuse to stay off the road whenever possible.

As a friend, I could appreciate why Jeff was moving in this direction. At the club, he didn't have to worry about the record companies or, for that matter, our organization. But when you're an entity, as Jeff definitely was, the problems that you're trying to avoid come from other directions. Once Healey's began getting some buzz, investors came in and persuaded Jeff to open a new place called Jeff Healey's

Roadhouse, in a prime location, across from Wayne Gretzky's restaurant and sports bar, where all the tourists gravitated. So even though Jeff thought he was liberating himself from the moneymen, he was just widening his sphere to include a new group of them.

Meanwhile, offers were still coming for the Jeff Healey Band from promoters all over the world. I tried to talk Jeff into touring a little while longer — maybe two years — so we could pay off our debts, wind down the company and live the rest of our lives as wealthy men. Joe liked the stage and would have gone along with the plan if Jeff was interested. And Jeff *was* willing to play select gigs for the right fee. Yet, he made clear, he no longer enjoyed rock 'n' roll — and had no intention of being stuck on a tour bus with Joe and I for months on end.

Then there was the issue of the album we were supposed to release on Atlantic. All that jazz stuff was well and good, but we'd made a commitment. I knew I was playing the heavy, bearing down on everyone to stay focused, but we were supposed to be making a record for Ahmet Ertegun. "You know who this guy is," I told Jeff. "We just can't fuck him."

Once again, we brought on Rich Chycki as an engineer. "They went through a lot of writers and a lot of producers," he says. "(Grammy-winning mix engineer) Michael Brauer came in, and then they weren't happy with the mixes, so they tossed them. It was huge money, you know? But that's how I ended up mixing the album."

If Rich was alone in the studio and noticed gaps in the songs, he had no qualms about picking up a rhythm guitar or playing percussion and mixing it in. And we trusted his judgment. He'd been around us for a long time, and could see through any veneer of bullshit we tried to put up. He noticed that we were a different kind of band than we'd been in the past.

"There was a lot of business stuff going on," he remembers. "The attitude of *hey, it's rock 'n' roll, we're having fun* wasn't there. It was work.

"I could sense that Jeff wasn't particularly interested in doing a record. But the band had an advance from the record company — a pretty good advance, I assume — and there was pressure to deliver a product. The pressure from the record company goes to management. And management happened to be the drummer.

"Jeff would come in, he would do his thing and he would just leave. His interest was waning, and that would rile Tom up. It's really fulfilling when you have an artist be into his own recording, and Jeff wasn't into the album that much. It was different from earlier albums, when everybody wanted to be together in the studio. By the time we got to this record, nobody wanted to be in the studio. You could feel everything starting to come undone."

Atlantic gave us two years to write and produce our album. When it wasn't delivered, I was the one who had to talk to Val Azzoli about our status with the company. He passed me to a business affairs lawyer.

"You ever watch the *Rocky and Bullwinkle* show?" he began.

"The cartoon? With the moose and the squirrel?"

"Well, you call him a squirrel. I call him a glorified rat."

I could see where this conversation was headed.

"You remember there was a part of the show where they'd have a parade?" the lawyer continued.

I knew exactly what he was talking about. In between segments, the *Rocky and Bullwinkle* theme music would be playing as various characters marched across the television screen with confetti streaming down.

"You see all kinds of people in that parade, right? Well, think of the ones at the front as our top artists. Then think of the ones in the middle as the up-and-coming artists. Then, at the end of the parade, there's a janitor sweeping up. Do you remember him?"

"Yeah. I do."

"You remember the janitor, then?"

"Yes."

"You're behind *that* guy."

In other words, we were off the label.

Not too long after that, we flew to the Montreux Jazz Festival for a performance; an album of the concert would be released, long after our band broke up, in 2005. Jeff was in his element, and once again we were having a good time. Bette Midler approached Jeff and said, "I know you can't see me, but I'm a big fan." He reached forward to hug her, but she was so short, he found himself embracing the air.

"Not only can I not see you," he cracked, "I can't feel you."

By circumstance, Ahmet Ertegun happened to be at the festival, as well. It was the first time he'd ever seen us play live, and he was impressed enough to come backstage afterwards and tell us how much he enjoyed the show. He and Jeff immediately realized that they shared many of the same interests, and began talking about record collecting and early 20th-century artists. I was standing there, smiling diplomatically, when Ertegun leaned over and said, "I can't wait to get your next record out."

"What do you mean?" I asked. "We've been dropped from the label."

Ertegun seemed confused. "Really? Who dropped you?"

By the time the business day started the next morning, I was informed that we were being re-signed.

It was a reprieve we needed. For the first time in a while, I was feeling confident. Jeff legitimately liked Ahmet, and I was hoping that might motivate him to shift his attention to the record.

One night, Jeff told me, he was hanging out with Ahmet and Eric Clapton in the studio, discussing great recordings of the past. Jeff and Clapton got into a dialogue over whether a certain record existed — while Ahmet sat back, taking it in. The night ended at 6 a.m. But two hours later, Jeff woke me up and demanded I drive him out to some barn owned by a record collector. As soon as we arrived, he began barking orders. We needed to scour the place, he said, until we found that fuckin' record. When we did, he was ecstatic. He later sent the record to Ahmet — as proof of his musical acumen.

I'm pretty sure that Ahmet was appreciative. Had we finished our album, I have no doubt that he would have seen to it that Atlantic made us a priority. Who knows? With that kind of a push, we might have had another *See the Light* on our hands. Unfortunately, Jeff continued to procrastinate. And he managed to alienate Ahmet by telling him that, even when the album was completed, he was too busy to tour for another year or so.

Well, if we weren't going to step up for Ahmet Ertegun, he wasn't going to kill himself for us, either. Looking at it objectively, we needed him a lot more than he needed the Jeff Healey Band.

We were dropped again — and this time, there wouldn't be a stay of execution.

nineteen

Remarkably, the Jeff Healey Band came out with one more album, *Get Me* *Some*, in 2000. Although the record was released by Universal in Canada and the independent Eagle Rock label in Europe, much of the music was the result of the labor we put in while I was trying to push Jeff to do that album for Ahmet Ertegun.

As I mentioned previously, on our earlier LPs we were frustrated because we didn't get to write enough original material. Now we fell into the opposite trap — writing *too many* of the songs on *Get Me* *Some*. All three of us had reached the point where we believed our own press. So instead of hiring ringers who had a better understanding of the formula needed to get a hit song on the radio, we gave ourselves more autonomy than we deserved. Even when we found a good cowriter, the band was in such disarray that we sometimes didn't realize what we had in front of us.

"In hindsight, I think the band was pressuring themselves in a lot of ways that they really didn't need to," Rich Chycki says. "It was a difficult time. There were a lot of people weighing in — a lot of cooks. That's one of the reasons Tom wanted me in the studio. I understood the band, and I could take all the different pieces they did and make it into one consistent album. But it was a fairly big task."

Yet the substance of the music was what it had always been. "Jeff would never lay down something that was substandard or pedestrian," Chycki said. "He was always a consummate musician. There's one song on the album called 'I Tried.' When he came in and picked up the guitar, he wasn't in the best spirits. And then he just played this ridiculously amazing solo. The song you hear on the album isn't cut together. It's a testament to Jeff as a musician. He could block out all that flotsam going on in the background, and lay down a solo of that quality — one of those things that would have been a great solo in 1975, 1995, 2005, 2025. You can't date it.

"It was sad because you'd walk up to him and say, 'Fuck. That was amazing.' And he would just go out and smoke, and then he would leave."

Our old friend Stevie Salas came in to help with the writing. Sometimes it was just he and I working out new material with session musicians. Jeff was concentrating on jazz. Maybe Joe was at his cottage in the country. Then, when Jeff came in, he'd listen to the demo. If there was something that captured his interest, he'd take it to the next level.

One of the songs Jeff particularly liked was "My Life Story." "They were a corporate band at this point," Stevie says. "You rarely worked with all three band members at the same time. I had a melody, some chords and some lyrics. Jeff sat down and when he heard my riff, he played it back exactly the way I played it. I'd sing a few words, and he'd type onto his braille machine, and sing the exact same phrase back. Maybe it was his lack of sight. Maybe it was just him. But his brain was so evolved.

"Jeff heard the notes and thought about and chose the notes differently than the rest of the great ones. At first, I thought this was because of his blues and jazz roots, but it was more than that. It was as if his mind saw notes floating around hiding in the shadows that none of us could see.

"I was really happy with the way 'My Life Story' was going. It was such a good song. Then Jeff brought in some producer who started changing shit around. So it left a bad taste in my mouth. We had all the elements we needed. But, as often happens in the music business, some guy who's not that talented comes in and starts division and fucks things up. I've never even heard the finished version."

As with our other albums, there's very little I'm ashamed of on *Get Me Some*. But, given our circumstances at the time, the album didn't do that well. There was no worldwide concert series to promote the record, and the little bit of touring we did wasn't moving us anywhere.

Obviously, I was now the pushy asshole, holding on to a lost dream and forcing Jeff to play gigs he didn't want. I have to thank the McDonald's restaurant chain for assisting me. I'm not sure I could have persuaded Jeff to go anywhere if McDonald's hadn't expanded internationally.

But in Europe our fans still wanted to see us, as Tony Tobias had predicted years earlier. During a tour of Germany, 80 percent of the tickets for our shows were sold. I knew that a little bit of publicity could push us to 100 percent, so I arranged for a national newspaper to do a story about us. When the photographer arrived before one of our concerts, I walked over to Joe and said that we were going to take a picture.

"Why didn't you tell me about this before? The wardrobe's all packed up. We don't have our makeup . . ."

I smiled, convinced he was joking. The Jeff Healey Band had never cared about makeup and wardrobe; as I mentioned, Jeff hated that stuff. And it's not like we had a hit record to draw people to our gigs. A little bit of publicity could go a long way.

But Joe was pissed off, so I said, "Let's go to Jeff" — like two feuding brothers going to Daddy.

Jeff listened to both of us, then turned to me. "You should have told Joe," he reprimanded.

What both of them were really saying was, "Fuck you, Tom." Or, more specifically, "Fuck the band," since the story never ran. No picture. No story.

As if it couldn't get worse, our relationship with Eagle Rock almost blew apart in Ottawa when one of their executives came on the tour bus and made an anti-Semitic crack, in earshot of Joe, who was Jewish. Now, honestly, Joe wasn't my favorite guy in the world at that time. But even at that putrefied phase of the Jeff Healey Band's history, I still had a "one for all and all for one" attitude. So I stood up and crowded the guy and told him, "You talk to my bass player like that, you're talking to all of us. So get the fuck off this bus before I throw you through the front window, you fuckin' asshole."

The guy left, then came back a minute later, claiming that the whole thing was a misunderstanding, and telling me that he was sorry.

"Well, don't apologize to me. Apologize to Joe."

He extended his hand to me while looking over at Joe. As I accepted the hand, I also shifted my gaze, to see how Joe would react. When I did, this jerk headbutted me in the face, busting open my nose.

I threw myself at the guy, and we tumbled out the door of the bus. But I ended up on top of him and holding him down in the snow. As he thrashed around below me, he cracked his knee, and had to hobble away when the fight was over.

Looking back on it, I don't remember Joe — the great martial artist — coming to my aid. In fact, I'm not even sure he thanked me. But I'm still proud of what I did. In fact, the only part about the

Like my boxing hero George Chuvalo, who went the distance with Muhammad Ali twice, I tried to always get off the canvas. CREDIT: TONY TOBIAS

incident I regret is looking away from the guy before his headbutt. If I could do the whole thing over, I'd have thrown the first punch.

So now I had a broken nose. But it kind of worked in our favor. When Eagle Rock found out the details, they paid for my nose job, fired the executive and kicked in extra marketing money. This had been the story of my life, back in the Maritimes and in the record business — talking when I should have been ducking. But I'd learned that if you keep saying "fuck it" and get up every time you're knocked down, you'll eventually get what you want. Technically, I'm not sure if I ever won a fight. I just kept getting up until the other guy was worn out.

"If Tom thought someone was being disrespected, he was always ready to get into a fight," said Stevie Salas. "He'd defend any woman, even a woman he didn't know. We were at a party in Laurel Canyon and this big gorilla of a guy — a bodyguard/bouncer type we'd see around — was walking through the room. Some girl got in his way, and this big monster just picked her up and threw her. She hit the wall and the couch, but nobody wanted to fuck with this guy, except Tom. Tom just charged at him and started punching him, and this guy was about two feet taller. But he didn't do anything. I think he looked up to Tom because he was in the Jeff Healey Band. And Tom kept hitting him and saying, 'Don't ever treat a woman like that again.'"

I sometimes compare my time in the Jeff Healey Band to my grandfather's stint during World War I — when he was buried in a bomb crater and managed to dig himself out. But there was little I could do to rescue us after Jeff did a television interview, belittling the music on *Get Me Some*. As with Clive and Ahmet and Val Azzoli, Jeff had left the executives at Universal in Canada no choice but to dump us.

He offered neither Joe nor I any apologies. He told journalist Jeff Hightower that Joe and I "always wanted to be superstars. And I never did. And yet, it was the Jeff Healey Band. So it was kind of counterproductive for them. They should have gone with somebody who, like them, wanted to be in that sort of phony, incredulous world of adulation that may or may not be genuine and so forth. And it's just ridiculous."

Describing his time as our front man, he reduced the experience as an endless blur of shows followed by excessive drinking "in order to sleep and get to the next show and play and get horrendously drunk. And that became such a treadmill that people die from."

Well, applying that criteria, Jeff's problems were solved. For all intents and purposes, the Jeff Healey Band was over.

twenty

I don't want to dwell on the negative. Some of the happiest times of my life were spent in the Jeff Healey Band, and I'd like to think that Jeff and Joe would have agreed. Yes, the three-person dynamic was difficult. One day, Jeff would think Joe was a jackass and I was a great guy. The next day, the situation would be reversed. We were constantly being questioned about the logic behind managing ourselves. But that wasn't always bad, because in some ways it brought us closer together. In my mind, we truly were a family. And families can be fucked up. It really didn't get horrible until the end.

Once Universal dropped us, Jeff and I were no longer bandmates. This wasn't true of Jeff and Joe. For a year or so afterwards, the two continued to perform together, often with other musicians, until Jeff fired him.

"I thought it would be easy after Tom," says agent Ralph James. "But now I was dealing directly with Jeff. First I had Tom, and Tom was a pain in the ass. Now I had Tom, Part II."

Although Jeff's repertoire still included a healthy ration of our songs, he rarely bypassed an opportunity to diminish our band. He spoke about the emancipation of not having to play songs just to satisfy a record label. "I suppose, left to my own devices, I wouldn't have done what I ended up doing from the late '80s through the '90s," he said in his interview with Jeff Hightower. "About four-fifths of what I did through there, I'm not too happy with anyway." It was jazz, he emphasized, "that I look at as real music."

Remember, this is the same guy who boasted about "making rock 'n' roll that's honest and unique, with the amp up enough to give you a jolt."

From the way Jeff was talking now, though, you'd think he'd never want to have anything to do with me again. Oddly, this wasn't the case. Even when he was trashing everything from my musical tastes to management skills, we remained friendly. One night, out of the blue, both Joe and I were invited to Jeff's club for a one-night reunion to celebrate the band's anniversary. I'm not going to lie and say that we were best friends. But there was both an acknowledgment of our shared history, and a respect for each other's abilities. Occasionally, he'd call and invite me to a venue to see a performer he'd discovered. "This kid's pretty good," he'd say. "You might want to sign him."

I took that to mean that Jeff still believed in my abilities as a manager.

Here's another weird thing. Despite how much Jeff claimed to hate the road, he was more than willing to front another group of musicians, play our songs and tour Europe, sometimes advertising the gigs with posters featuring pictures of Joe and I. It was a little bit of a kick in the head. The same guy who said our music sucked, at the very least, was going through the motions to make a buck.

Steve Herman, the agent we'd met when we were trying to score college gigs before our first record deal, hired Jeff to open a club he'd purchased with some partners in Sudbury, Ontario. "By this point, I'd known Jeff for almost 20 years," Steve says. "We agreed on a price — $10,000 or something — for him to play, and everyone seemed very excited. Just before he's supposed to go on, he turns to me and says, 'Steve, I'm not going onstage unless you give me the cash right now.' So I run around Sudbury in 20-below to find a bank machine to get Jeff his money.

"It was sad. He wasn't the same person I'd known before. He'd developed this distrust. I've seen it happen with lots of musicians. Over time, they don't trust anyone. They think they're being screwed by everybody. And sometimes they are. But sometimes they're not."

Steve also noticed something that never happened with the Jeff Healey Band. Jeff was struggling to connect with his audience, possibly because the business of negotiation was taking a toll on his artistic spirit. "Some people are better at one thing than another," Steve says. "Jeff was used to Tom being the businessman and running everything, and I guess he wanted to prove that he could be a businessman, too. But he probably would have furthered himself better by just focusing on music."

In 2003, after more than eight thousand cases of the respiratory disease SARS were reported in 37 countries, the Stones — now on the tail end of their *40 Licks* tour — announced that they were coming back to Toronto to headline a Stars for SARS concert at Downsview Park. As soon as I heard about it, I called Jeff and tried to sell him on putting the band back together for one night. Even when he seemed uninterested, I argued that a show of this magnitude in Jeff's hometown demanded his presence.

"The Jeff Healey Band doesn't have to play if you don't want us to," I said. "But *Jeff Healey* should play. I don't even care if we have to put a band together around you."

I knew from Steve Herman that Sass Jordan, who had three Juno awards for Best Female Vocalist of the year, was going to be featured on the show. Steve suggested that during her performance, she bring up Jeff for a couple of songs. Sass loved the idea, and I was satisfied taking a backseat role, watching their two great voices mesh in front of five hundred thousand fans.

"It was really uncomfortable backstage," remembers Stevie Salas. "I brought Tom to the show; he was my guest. And it was really weird between Tom and Jeff. You could tell that the new people around Jeff really didn't like Tom. They were trying to move Jeff in a new direction, and Jeff was letting himself be isolated. It was a bummer. I knew how the guys in the Jeff Healey Band loved each other. They'd fight, but they loved each other. And I don't give a fuck who gets offended by this — these new people had no idea what these guys had. They weren't there. And now Tom was the enemy.

"It was like Dean Martin and Jerry Lewis. It was a love story. And nothing bad really happened. Nobody stole from anybody else. Nobody fucked anyone else's wife. It was all insinuation. And that fucked everything up."

Jeff was cordial to me backstage, but not overly warm. Nonetheless, when I introduced him to one of my new artists, he told her that she had a good manager.

Just before he was supposed to go on, I noticed that nobody in his entourage had bothered to request that a chair be placed onstage for Jeff. So I asked Jeff if he needed one.

"Yeah. Thanks a lot."

I grabbed a chair, found a roadie and handed it to him — just as I would have done in the old days.

Once the concert ended, Jeff went back to his other interests. He had a new jazz band, the Jazz Wizards, playing trumpet and guitar, along with piano and drums when the mood struck him. So he obviously didn't need me around. As always, he preferred improvising onstage, specializing in a style of music often referred to as Dixieland. Yet, when a reporter from the Canoe.com entertainment site made the mistake of uttering this characterization, Jeff was quick to correct him: "Dixieland is a state of mind, not a form of music. You get visions of hats and canes, which is kind of distressing to those of us who appreciate good music."

He'd also started his own jazz label and was hosting a radio show on the CBC called *My Kinda Jazz*. When people asked about his affinity for older music, he pointed out that oldies stations still drew large audiences and no one seemed to have a problem with that. In fact, he argued, the songs on those stations evolved from the jazz and blues from three or four decades earlier. Jeff's conclusion: the current commercial offerings were just watered-down, over-produced hybrids of the stuff he'd been enjoying since childhood — and far less interesting.

This is a position I'll never dismiss. Jeff was the most astute musicologist I ever met, and the people who listened to his radio show always received an education. After all these years, Jeff was still going out to flea markets like an archeologist sifting through dirt and ash with a sieve, uncovering his version of the Dead Sea Scrolls. One time, at a sale in Mississauga, he found a series of book album sets with records that had never been played — 78s that had passed from the manufacturer to the dealer but were never sold.

Because Jeff had achieved sobriety and wasn't living the same rock 'n' roll lifestyle, he had more time to work as a representative for the Canadian National Institute for the Blind — the organization Keith Richards helped subsidize with his benefit concert after his drug bust — promoting braille literacy and other projects that meant a lot to him.

In 2004, he and his jazz trio played at McMaster University in Hamilton, Ontario, as part of a ceremony that saw Jeff receive an honorary doctorate of letters. I wasn't there, but I can imagine the half smirk he must have had on his face as he stood there in his mortarboard cap and told the university's president, "It's good to be a doctor."

Some people dwell on these tales to depict Jeff as something of a saint. I knew the full person, including the part of Jeff that could be as devious as anyone else. But none of his efforts were false. He truly cared about the blind, and the role of music in uplifting society and inspiring children. And if that makes him a little bit saintly, well, as a lapsed Catholic myself, I can tell you that there were far less worthy candidates who've been canonized.

Some people may be surprised to read this, given the tension that we experienced later on, but I sincerely believe that Jeff's second wife, Cristie Hall, was a major factor in encouraging his charitable impulses.

Jeff met Cristie when she was working at his club. She was a singer in his jazz and blues band, as well. They married in 2003 and had a son two years later. I never met the boy, but I read that he was born with retinoblastoma, the same condition as Jeff's. When he was 18 months old, doctors found a dozen tumors in his eyes. Fortunately, there were more options than when Jeff was a kid. His son received proactive laser and freezing treatments. Four years later, according to a CBC report, he was not only tumor-free but didn't even wear glasses.

It made me think about Jeff. If he'd been born later, I wonder about whether his vision would have been saved, as well as the kind of life he might have had.

As part of Jeff's self-improvement campaign, he decided to give up drinking. I've done this a couple of times, but admit I enjoy imbibing too much to deprive myself permanently. Jeff was in a different frame of mind. He never intended to drink again. He joined Alcoholics Anonymous, I later heard, and began attending meetings. Through this process, he began to view me as someone who enabled his bad habits. To be fair, I think he was being a little too generous on that point — I not only enabled Jeff when it came to drinking, I *encouraged* him. Either way, he largely cut off communication with me, something that both baffled and hurt. I actually wish he'd confronted me, told me how he felt and explained why we could no longer be friends. If I'd known that's what he had to do to maintain his sobriety, I would have accepted it.

People told me that he also wrote some hateful comments about me on the internet. The post was apparently only up for two or three hours. By the time I learned about his remarks and went searching for them, they'd been taken down. So I never read Jeff's words, only heard about them. But here's the weird thing. A few weeks later, he called me out of the blue, just to see what was going on. We had a short, friendly conversation. Then he cut me off again.

During the last few years that we were touring, I remember seeing Jeff have trouble walking before the show. I assumed this was the result of all the jumping around onstage. I also knew that, once the lights went up, he'd forget about his pain and put on an incredible show. But, more and more, he seemed to be wiped out once the music ended.

In 2005, I learned what was *really* wrong with Jeff when he had two cancerous sarcomas removed from his legs. If anything was a sobering realization, this was. Maybe Jeff was so cranky, and so intent on staying close to home, because he was dying.

Like I've said before, during the height of the Jeff Healey Band years, we were gods among men. But to whom the gods give, they also take away. On our song "One Foot on the Gravel," Jeff sang about always having one foot in the grave. He knew. He knew his life was not going to be a long one.

When I'd tell Jeff to eat more greens, he'd treat me like an idiot. He'd smoke two packs a day and not worry about contracting emphysema 20 or 25 years in the future. In the back of his mind, I'm convinced, he understood his destiny.

Once in a while, we still managed to talk. Sometimes it was awkward. Sometimes it was friendly. Sometimes it was businesslike. The last time we met was not pleasant. He called a meeting in which he told me, flat out, that he no longer cared about our music and wanted no association with it whatsoever.

His 2007 interview with Jeff Hightower summed up his attitude at the time: "I find it laughable, frankly, that festivals internationally will pay so much money for me and other old-timers to trot out their old material when I'm sure most of the others, like myself, are sick of it. You kind of want to move on to other things. Some are not. Some are so happy to get the constant adulation it seems to bring, as hard to believe as it is . . . that they want to play their past material over and over."

I was confused by the rant. I knew that he wanted to preserve his integrity as a jazz artist. But, one-on-one, we could sometimes find neutral ground. "If you really feel that way," I told him, "I don't know why you're still out there, playing our music with other musicians."

He refused to look at my logic. "I don't give a fuck about the music," he said. "I don't give a fuck about the band. It's not something I care about."

It was then that he offered *me*, Tom Stephen, the publishing rights to the Jeff Healey Band catalog.

"In 2005, I was with Jeff and his new band at a festival in Sweden," says Ben Richardson, the bass player for our opening band, the Phantoms. "Jeff was hardly playing his own songs. And sometimes he'd tell the guys in his band, 'I hate singing. You sing the next song.' I remember they played 'Highway to Hell,' and he made (keyboardist) Dave Murphy sing — to twenty thousand people who came to hear Jeff Healey sing a song. Jeff's jumping around onstage and Dave has this look on his face, like, 'What the fuck am I doing?' People would shout out requests for 'Angel Eyes,' and Jeff would say, right over the microphone, 'I'm not playing that shit.'

"My girlfriend was doing sound for Jeff, and I was doing monitors at the festival. Jeff and I were sitting at this picnic table offstage and we both had to use the bathroom, so we went over by these trees to piss. We're both standing there, pissing, and Jeff says, 'Yo, Ben, I think I'm going to give Tom everything. He's on my back (about back taxes and the logistics of winding up the company) and I don't want to have anything to do with it anymore.'

"I was flabbergasted. 'What are you talking about Jeff? That's crazy. That's a lot of money and your legacy, and you want to give it away?' But he was adamant that he'd be happy to get rid of it all. Years later, my best friend and Jeff's future bass player and producer Alec Fraser, told me that he had had the *exact* same conversation with Jeff."

Despite the fact that I'd later be described as a money grabber who swiped the rights away from a dying man, the truth is that I tried to reason with Jeff about taking the cut he deserved. "It doesn't matter if you don't like the music anymore," I said. "You have two kids. This is your legacy. Don't you want to give something to them?"

At this stage, I was conscious that he might not live to be a hundred. "You can't just throw the publishing away."

"I don't give a fuck," he shot back. "I'm doing my own thing. You want the publishing. It's yours. That's what I'm telling you, Tom. I'm being fair to you. You care about this shit. I don't. Take it or leave it."

On August 26, 2005, the two of us officially broke up in the office of entertainment accountant Jae Gold, a member of the Canadian Academy of Recording Arts and Sciences, which runs the Juno Awards. "The band was cash-flow-challenged and fighting, and that's when they came to me as a client," says Jae. "I was just trying to get them friends again to the point that it could be an amicable divorce.

"I liked all three guys. Joe Rockman was a great guy. Tom was Tom. Jeff, of course, was so talented and interesting. Jeff obviously wanted nothing to do with this stuff anymore. He didn't want to tour with the band, didn't like rock 'n' roll. He was exhausted, drained. He didn't give a shit.

"The whole agreement was two paragraphs. Jeff was relinquished from all responsibilities, except for a $59,027.00 tax liability that he eventually paid. The second paragraph read, 'Ownership of all publishing rights regarding the music of the Jeff Healey Band and all masters and tapes, video, film are the property of Tom Stephen.'

"You can't get much clearer than that. Jeff and Tom signed the agreement in front of me. Joe signed by fax. This is what Jeff wanted."

I don't know how much time Jeff spent considering his mortality. But I wonder whether he thought, with the end in sight, that he needed to purge his soul by disassociating himself from any blood money tied to the record business. It doesn't make a lot of sense to me. But it was what it was.

In the years to come, I'd frequently feel that it was a mistake to accept Jeff's offer. By signing the agreement, I set myself up as a target. People have called me a liar, a thief and a con man. But Jeff was probably right. I guess, at that time, I really *did* care about the music — and the Jeff Healey Band — more than he did.

twenty-one ——————

I'm not proud of everything I did during my time in the Jeff Healey Band.
But whenever I hear one of our songs, I flush with pride. That's *me*
playing the drums behind the best blues guitar player ever born.

There were new people in Jeff's world now, guys like Alec Fraser,
who played in the band at Jeff's club and engineered his jazz albums.
Clearly, he cared about Jeff the way Joe and I had. In an interview
with TheBluegrassSpecial.com, Alec spoke about a conversation he
had with Jeff, trying to persuade him to consider alternative treatments for his cancer. "He says to me, 'Look, Alec, everybody's got to
get on board with this. There's no cure for what I have. It's a matter
of time. Obviously, I'm going to hang around for as long as I can for
the sake of everyone.' He was thinking of his family."

Jeff intended to keep playing until the end. In 2006, he made a deal with a German blues label, Ruf Records, to do another album. He booked summer festival dates months in advance. He said that, even if he died, he wanted his bandmates to tour and support the record. When Alec questioned how it would be possible to do a Jeff Healey gig without Jeff Healey, he was met with the type of illogical answer that used to drive me nuts: "A gig is a gig."

One night in 2007, my phone rang, and there was Jeff on the other end. "Hey, Jeff," I said, with a bit of anxiety. "What's going on?"

He started talking about a website for one of his projects, and asked my opinion about the content and the overall theme.

I answered as best I could, then asked how he was doing.

"Okay."

"Heard you hadn't been doing so well."

Jeff evaded the question. He paused, then said, "How are *you* doing, Tom?"

"I'm doing okay." There was silence on the line. The mood was very dark. I was trying to think of something I could say to reconnect us.

"Well, you know, Jeff, it'd be good to get together sometime."

"Yeah, we'll see what happens."

That was pretty much it. I wouldn't characterize the call as a reconciliation. But at least it wasn't hostile. I'm not sure if he was trying to let me know he still considered me a friend, or trying to create his own peace of mind so he could go out without any hard feelings.

In the days and weeks after our conversation, I was pretty broken up and found myself replaying it over and over in my mind, hoping for some subtle sign in the clumsy dialogue that we were still connected as brothers. Look — I might be a crazy musician. I might have a lot of things wrong with me. But I valued our friendship and just wanted things to be normal between us, so I could support Jeff while he struggled through the last days of his life.

When I found out that his cancer had spread to his lungs, I was really scared. At the time, my sister was also battling cancer. It was a fight she'd eventually lose, but at the time she was feeling optimistic. I wanted Jeff to know that, even after my sister's cancer had spread, she'd been able to persevere. So I phoned Joe to pass on a message.

"Joe, Jeff knows what my sister's been going through, and I've been spending a lot of time talking to her about Jeff. She says no one can really encourage a cancer patient like another cancer patient. So please let Jeff know that if he wants to talk to my sister, I'd love to arrange it."

I never heard anything back, but I didn't rule out the possibility of getting another phone call when I least expected one. Some more time passed. Then a buddy on the music scene called and said, "Look, Jeff's in really bad shape. And the odds of him making it are worse than ever before. Some people are saying he's got weeks, maybe days. Maybe hours."

I immediately called Joe again. But Joe was nowhere to be found. For the next 24 or 48 hours — I can't remember the time frame — all my time was spent trying to get a hold of people with information about Jeff.

Finally, on March 2, 2008, Joe left me a long, sad, horrible message. Jeff was dead.

Session musician Steve Lukather spoke to Jeff the night before he died. "I called him at the hospital," Steve says. "I called and he answered. He sounded weak. I told him I loved him, and, trying not to be negative, said I'd see him soon. But he knew and I knew.

"It just wasn't fair. There'll never be another like him. He showed the world that music will get out of the soul one way or another, that there's no *wrong* way to play an instrument or make music. His musical voice will live forever."

When I called Joe back, we spent the next two hours going around, reliving our experiences, with Joe uttering the same thing over and over: "We're the only two guys left. You don't appreciate things 'til they're gone. We have to move on from whatever misunderstandings we had in the band, and stay friends. It's up to us to look after our legacy. We have to do this for Jeff."

I didn't remember feeling that bonded with Joe since the night the three of us had decided to form the band.

But the closeness didn't last. In fact, I was told — from a friend of a friend — that I wouldn't be welcome at the funeral. That was crushing, because the least I could do, after all that Jeff and I had been through, was show my respects to his family. Yet I was warned, "Don't even show up outside the church." So I couldn't even go as a fan.

My assumption is that this decree came from the widow, who, I surmised, may have had an exaggerated view of Jeff's dislike for me. After all, she and I didn't even know each other.

My feelings wavered from heartbroken to angry. At one point, I thought, "Fuck it. Jeff was my friend. I'm going." And then I thought about Jeff's father, Bud, and how he must have been suffering. The last thing I was going to do was cause a scene and disrespect him — not to mention Jeff's kids.

Meanwhile, I was getting call after call from people who wanted to talk about Jeff, and I was certainly in no mood to tell them that I wasn't going to the funeral. So I got on a plane to New York, where a friend had an empty apartment. For three days, I locked myself inside, reliving the time I first saw Jeff onstage, him driving that bus on the icy highway, the bowling game he won against the members of ZZ Top, our conversations about the way he "saw" colors in his mind. I was so sad about a brilliant talent leaving the world too soon, as well as the way our friendship ended. And I felt guilty, too, thinking that maybe if I hadn't pushed him to be a rock star, he might still be alive. Because I believe that stress has an impact on your health. And after fighting with me for the last few years of the Jeff Healey Band, he took on the added burden of handling his own business affairs, and I'm sure that wore him down.

There'd be times when I'd fall into a fitful sleep and wake up, thinking that I felt better. On one of those occasions, I left the apartment to get a newspaper. When I opened the *New York Times*, there was Jeff's obituary.

I ran back upstairs and locked myself in again.

Eventually, I had to return to Toronto, where people were still mourning the loss of their native son. There was a series of concerts, organized by Jeff's wife and fellow musicians. One raised money for Daisy's Eye Cancer Fund, an organization dedicated to fighting retinoblastoma, the disease that claimed Jeff's vision. The fund had been started by the parents of a British girl after they traveled to Canada and their daughter's last functioning eye was saved at Toronto's Hospital for Sick Children. The Jazz Wizards played, along with other people Jeff knew. Local musician Dave Murphy led Healey's House Band in renditions of Jeff's favorite jazz songs from the 1920s and '30s. Joe was an active participant. But again, I was told to stay away.

I did as I was asked, and I'm sure a lot of people interpreted my absence at these important events as a sign of not caring. It hasn't been until now that I've been able to put the whole story in context.

About a month after the funeral, Alberta-based Stony Plain Records released *Mess of Blues*, a combination of Jeff's more recent recordings, with the estate's blessing. When I attempted to release *Legacy: Volume One*, a triple-disc DVD/CD collection, a few months later on Winnipeg's Arbor Records, Cristie Healey urged fans to boycott the project since, by her estimation, it "didn't honor Jeff's memory." According to the widow, my goal was to "exploit Jeff's name."

A couple of thousand units had already been sold. But because of the attack, the label and wholesalers became nervous. In a sworn affidavit, Cristie Healey insisted that the estate owned the rights to the Jeff Healey Band's music. She'd later concede in another affidavit that this wasn't true, but the label had no desire to go to war with the widow of a blind Canadian icon who'd tragically lost his life at 41.

What no one was saying was that I'd actually gone to the estate's lawyers before the release with an offer of 20 percent of the proceeds. If you calculate in Jeff's writing shares, the proceeds would have been in the neighborhood of 50 percent. I didn't do this out of guilt. I knew how much Jeff valued his family and thought it was only right that the earnings be shared with them. The offer was rejected.

I should have known then that the estate's attitude would be all or nothing.

The *Legacy: Volume One* project was halted, and from this point forward, Tom Stephen became a pariah. It was the beginning of a jail sentence for a crime I'd never committed. People avoided me. While I was able to make deals on behalf of several Canadian artists in the United States, in my own country I was toxic.

I exiled myself from the Canadian music industry. Yet even then, I was shocked at how much damage innuendo could do. My mother, siblings, nieces and nephews all read articles implying that I'd taken advantage of Jeff. I chose not to fight back, because I respected Jeff and our history. It would not dignify anyone to feud over my late friend's carcass.

If Jeff were still alive, I'm convinced, we could have worked things out. Would he have called me names and questioned my motives in the media? That was Jeff. Might there have been a few letters sent back and forth from attorneys? Probably. But would anyone have pulled the trigger and gone to court? Absolutely not.

Jeff was so skilled at the art of insulting me, I think he got more satisfaction that way. It was almost like improvising a good jazz piece.

Eventually, I was forced to sell my rights to the Jeff Healey Band's assets to a company called MCW, which then sold the rights to the Eagle Rock label. Aware of the diamonds sitting in our vault, Eagle Rock commissioned me to curate material for future projects. Once again, I made overtures to the estate and was rebuffed. Joe and I met several times until he cut off contact with me. To this day, I don't know why.

In 2011, Eagle Rock released *Live at Grossman's*, the live concert we did in 1994 while we were putting together *Cover to Cover*, the first of what I'd hoped would be a series of box sets. But in the promotional material, someone made a grave error, describing *Live at Grossman's* as a project that the estate supported.

The timing couldn't have been worse. Eagle Rock was in the midst of negotiating a sale to Universal. Hoping to alleviate any controversy, Eagle Rock settled with the estate, throwing me under the bus. I understand their strategy, of course. Who would you rather alienate, Tom Stephen — a guy who, throughout his own book, admits that he can be an asshole — or the widow of — I'll say it again — a blind, dead Canadian idol?

In 2016, the estate released what it called our "lost album," *Heal My Soul*, in honor of Jeff's 50th birthday, on the Convexe Entertainment / Universal Music label — the same company, by the way, that dumped us after Jeff went on television and trashed the music on *Get Me Some*. "Not having even met Jeff at this point in his life," Cristie said in the liner notes, "the opportunity to hear this record in its entirety has added yet another piece to the wonderful man I knew and loved. I see these recordings as something very different from any rock release of Jeff's. There seems to be a different edge, emotion and passion."

The songs were written between 1996 and 1998, according to the liner notes, "a time of swirling emotional turmoil for Jeff Healey. A decade of non-stop touring and recording had left his personal life in disarray, and his band of 13 years was on the verge of coming apart at the seams."

Joe was quoted as remembering, "Relations strained during the time of these recordings, making things challenging beyond the norm to write, record and perform together. Our self-managed partnership that served well in early years to achieve record deals and [tour] the world started breaking down."

Ultimately, the notes continued, Jeff had no choice but to "fight back against years of growing mismanagement and frustration. With no regrets, Jeff walked away from that part of his musical life . . . to focus more fully on his other lifelong passion, traditional American jazz."

In addition to reminiscing in the liner notes about her romance with Jeff, Cristie was effusive in thanking the album's production coordinator, her current husband, Roger Costa — one-time owner of a vintage record shop in Toronto, and a friend of Jeff's — describing him as "my partner in everything, who I trusted to make this happen because I believed in your vision of what was possible."

"I first heard several of the key tracks on this release almost 20 years ago when Jeff played them for me," Roger told the Canadian music journal *FYI*. "They'd just been recorded, and he was very proud of his work . . . I always maintained that these were some of the strongest performances Jeff ever recorded, and hoped that we'd find the right home for them, so we could share them with the public."

If Jeff cherished this music so much, you'd have to wonder why we hesitated to release any of it — particularly when our label was pressuring us to get some new product out there. I might be biased, but I have a pretty vivid memory of this period, as well as Jeff's attitude about the songs.

He hated them.

"I'm credited with writing two songs on the album," says Ben Richardson, the former bassist for Toronto indie band, The Phantoms, "and I remember when the songs were recorded. They were our songs, and Tom talked Jeff into singing them. They were outtakes. I know Jeff definitely didn't want those songs ever released.

"At one point, I tried talking to the estate to help work out the differences they had with Tom. Roger sent me an email saying, 'We may passionately disagree with Tom on many issues and have very different opinions, but there is absolutely no intention to cause harm to Tom or ever disclose information that's untrue.' Then, two weeks later, we were on the phone and Roger said that he spoke to some record company guys who told him the story about Tom going down to New York to get the band their deal is a fabrication. I mean, I was around then. I knew what happened. And Roger also said that, early on, when each band member was working for a small salary, Tom was having his laundry delivered by limo. But those are the kinds of lies that were out there."

The estate claimed that, in compiling the album, "master tapes were meticulously restored, transferred, mixed and mastered.

Throughout the process, we sought to strip away any veneer of dated sounds and effects."

But something else was also stripped away. My drum parts are missing from 9 out of the 12 tracks on the album. I read that these were replaced by a drummer named Dean Glover — "an exceptional musician," according to Costa, "and dear friend" — sometimes while Joe hung out in the studio.

"Anybody is welcome to repurpose a song," says our former engineer Rich Chycki. "But taking a little eraser and just removing something just doesn't sit well. It feels like you're trying to say, 'Let's change the drummer and teach him a lesson.' It doesn't serve Jeff's legacy. You might pretend that the sessions with Tom on drums never happened. But they happened."

Here's how Costa addressed the issue: "Many of the songs had unfinished drum tracks," he told the *Good New Music* blog, "placeholder recordings, and even electronic drums in a couple of cases. It was quite common for whoever was around at the time to lay down a quick drum track for a song to be built on — sometimes even Jeff."

Once again, I remember it differently. There aren't too many protocols left to break on the perfidious rock 'n' roll landscape, but literally amputating a musician's contributions from a recording is one of them.

And here's something equally bizarre. Back when the pictures that accompany the album were taken, the entire Jeff Healey Band was photographed. But in the *Heal My Soul* artwork, you only see Jeff and Joe. It's as if Tom Stephen didn't exist, and my role as Jeff's bandmate, business partner and confidante is some fiction invented in my mind.

As we all know now, it isn't.

As I was finishing up this book, I received some disheartening news — I had a rare form of cancer. And I immediately thought of Jeff, and the way that stubborn fuck battled his own cancer and never gave up. He was a fighter and I'm a fighter. We were in it together and we were in it to win. And that's what I intend to do. Bizarrely, having this terrible disease made me realize that I understand Jeff possibly better than anyone else. His struggles and my struggles were the same back when the Canadian record labels wouldn't sign us, and they're the same today. Now I know why Jeff seemed so angry during his final years. He had cancer, man, and it sucked and he was pissed off.

I finally understand Jeff's fatalism. He'd been dealing with the stuff since he had his eyes removed as a kid, and knew this awful disease would come back. His destiny was written in his mind. But while he was on this earth, all that mattered was the music, great music. I wish I'd figured out the riddle that was Jeff sooner. Not that it would have changed many things. But, at least, I would have appreciated Jeff — and his artistry — in a different way.

In an interview with the *Toronto Star* in 2007, Jeff spoke about his cancer, and said, "I had 40 good years." That was Jeff — brave 'til the end.

At times, I can hear Jeff's voice in my head, challenging me, refusing to let me give in to self-pity or even the thought of defeat. And it motivates me even more to tell his story — our story — the right way, the way it really happened. If other people have a problem with it, fuck them. Because I know I'm telling the truth, and wherever Jeff is, he knows, too.

Jeff's death created a void that's never been filled for me. It's not like I need to feed off his fame — I've handled a number of artists' careers since my time in the Jeff Healey Band, and been involved with a series of multimedia projects — but I miss his humor, his insights into the world, his originality and his tenaciousness. Like a spouse who becomes widowed, I have to admit that, sometimes, I even miss fighting with Jeff.

I never got the chance to thank him for this. But if it wasn't for Jeff, I might be some boring old dude, still working as an urban planner, ripping up lawns and streets, building skyscrapers and fucking up the planet even more than it already is. Jeff Healey saved me from that world, and in a way, I owe him.

An interesting thing happened while I was researching the book.

I spent one night re-listening to our music. I didn't think about infighting or sadness or my issues with the estate, just the music, the way we loved each other, and the way the fans, in turn, loved us. And I fell in love with the Jeff Healey Band all over again.

Whether I was backing him onstage or listening at home, I was always invigorated by Jeff the performer. Every day, I miss his music, and believe that the world is a poorer place without Jeff creating new sounds. Not to mention the songs we recorded together that no one — outside the tight little circle surrounding the Jeff Healey Band — ever heard.

"It's sad because there's so much music that is unreleased," says Chycki. "I recorded tons and tons of jams, and tons and tons of songs that people should hear. Jeff was really a fantastic artist, as well as an unbelievable, magnanimous person. The world deserves both to hear his music and learn about Jeff the human being. There's a lot there that can inspire everyone."

If this book accomplishes one thing, I hope it encourages new fans to listen to Jeff's music — both the stuff that's already out there and the other songs that I know will be released one day. When I look into the future, I see a time when Jeff will be regarded as one of the true legends of blues, along with names like Robert Johnson, Lead Belly and Blind Lemon Jefferson. Because that's where he belongs.

I also imagine kids who are just starting to play music, listening to a Jeff Healey recording — or looking at a video of Jeff on YouTube, leaping out of his chair while running his big fingers over the guitar strings — and feeling motivated to pick up an instrument and do the same thing. The only comparison I can make is to Bob Dylan, who discovered Robert Johnson in the early '60s and, because of that experience, went on to write songs that changed the world.

It's reassuring to know that I'm far from the only person who feels this way. "Jeff could absolutely be rediscovered at any time," Paul Shaffer says, "because he was brilliant."

Brilliant — but, to a large extent, misunderstood. I hope you know him a little better now. I began writing this book because

I wanted to tell people about my own experiences in the band —
as well as the man who was Jeff Healey, a guy who was fair, rude,
contradictory, maddening, petty, a comedian, a genius, a brother, a
human who loved me and stood up for Joe and me. I can only hope I
did my best to reciprocate.

Despite my bout with cancer, I don't plan to die for a long time. No, I want to stay right here on earth, empowered by my memories of those days laughing and goofing off, setting up our own gear in shitty little clubs and freezing our asses off on cots in cheap motel rooms, swept up in the excitement and energy of moving our dream forward. Somehow, it's those recollections that have so much more resonance than the massive festivals, the TV appearances, the girls, the awards, the promises about big things to come. The promises meant so much more when they were the promises we made when we were alone — to each other, to ourselves.

Like I said at the beginning, we were three nerds who conquered the world — behind a guy who beat every conceivable odd on the planet, and never stopped being his own man, a guy who taught me about bravery and character and living life with fearlessness.

No matter what else was going on, Jeff was determined to never miss a show. And when he walked out onstage, he gave more than 10 men combined. Yeah, he was an opinionated son of a bitch, but he deserved to have his opinion because he was one of the greats.

Jeff Healey was the best musician I've ever known in my life. Period. By far. No one touches the guy. For 15 years of my life, I had the best seat in the house, backing him up both literally and figuratively.

It was a great ride. And now you know what it was like.

EPILOGUE

Writing this book has been an interesting journey, a series of highs and lows that were not unlike the ones described on the pages you just read. Writing a memoir teaches you a lot through hindsight. I'm no longer that cocky "go for it all" guy depicted in this book. (I guess we all mature to some extent.) And I'm not sure I realized how much the Jeff Healey Band continued to dominate my existence long after Jeff's premature departure from this world.

While I should have been able to enjoy the legacy I shared with Jeff, I've spent too much time dealing with lawyers and spurious allegations about my character and intentions. None of this was deserved. As I say throughout the book, like anyone, I can be a jerk; but I was the Jeff Healey Band's jerk, and I always believed in Jeff. Sadly, I'm fully confident that, by the time you read this book, certain

Flying to Halifax with Rob.

people will use its existence to depict me in the worst possible terms. It's been that way for so many years, I've come to regard it as normal.

I now realize that I was fighting with one hand behind my back. My respect for Jeff prevented me from fighting with the ferocity I was known for when battling for the band.

I am constantly amazed at what humans will do to each other over power, money and spite.

From the time I saw my father's business stolen out from under him — with the collusion of the banks and the courts — I always knew that the justice system was rigged. It's the same system that the estate has used to keep me in my place. This has cost me a lot — both financially and emotionally. Weird . . . for a guy who could get others to the top, I was struggling to look after myself. But a funny thing happened while I was getting my ass kicked. I discovered how great people can be. People like my immediate family, as well as Tony, Sam and Theresa, have been there from the beginning and never

Brothers in arms at Hubbards.
From left to right: Tom, Victor, Jordy and Mike.

let me down. Good friends like Dawna, Mischke, Stevie and Benno were always there to pick me up, dust me off and throw me back in the game. Through this process, I gained a good friend in Keith, the co-author of this book. Jacqui kept me technically together, which for those who know me is no small feat. And Susan, the owner of Catcha Falling Star in Negril, and my other good friends in Jamaica have not only been welcoming and supportive, but a refuge when other things seemed so dark.

The Halifax crew has been with me every day, even when they didn't know it. They are my crazy, interesting fellow music lovers from all walks of life. A couple days after a particular deal went south, I was told that I had cancer. Then, that I didn't have cancer. Then, finally, that I actually did have cancer. I was a little down. My friend Rob flew me on his jet to Halifax, where I was embraced by my many other friends there. Together, we got to see my lifetime favorite musician, Matt Minglewood, at Hubbards. While Rob put me up at his castle, we hung out with Victor, jammed at his club and had dinner with Jordy and Mike, who has been the de facto historian for this book. It may sound odd, and I know I was probably in shock, but it was one of the best times of my life. A friend of Rob's, Bruce, a complete stranger, then flew me back to Toronto and took me out for an amazing dinner with his doctor friend, who helped walk me through some of the challenges I'd be facing. I mean — what the hell? Not a bad way to start my fight. So, as our song said, "Maybe love is the answer" — or at least a weekend of partying with your buds.

A year later, while finishing the book, I returned to Halifax to attend our friend Rob's induction into the Nova Scotia Business Hall of Fame. We were all proud of Rob, and it was a great event. At a private party afterwards, Rob got up and introduced the band, Tom Cochrane and Red Rider. It was mind blowing; Tom is one of the greatest Canadian artists, who gave us such songs as "Life is a Highway" and "Big League," the unofficial anthem for Canadian hockey. In between songs, I was shocked when he started talking about Jeff Healey. He told a couple of good stories he heard from our mutual guitar tech, Gary Scrutton. Then, Tom posed this question for everyone to ponder: "Why isn't Jeff Healey in the fuckin' Rock 'n' Roll Hall of Fame?"

I was shocked but I shouldn't have been, since Tom had given our band its first major Canadian tour and did the same for Amanda Marshall. Backstage, we were both stunned to run into each other in Halifax. Over a few drinks, I told him about this book. He couldn't have been more supportive, and he gave me some great positive energy. Now you know why I keep going back to Halifax — a place that played a huge part in breaking the Jeff Healey Band.

To my friends and family, from day one, you know who you are and I love you all. None of us really know how things will end. But by being the best you can be, you've brought out the same in me. So, my philosophy now narrows down to this: be good to your friends and family and, as we used to say when we were kids, "Just keep on trucking."

I'll leave you with parting lyrics from one of the songs the Jeff
Healey Band performed:

I went back to the bar again
And headed straight for the band
I need to remember not to forget
All the life and the love we had . . .

TOM STEPHEN continues to work in artist management, dividing his time between Toronto, Los Angeles and Jamaica.

KEITH ELLIOT GREENBERG is a *New York Times* best-selling author and television producer who's written for *Maxim*, *Playboy*, the *New York Observer*, *Village Voice* and *USA Today*, among others. His credits include the autobiographies of pro wrestling icons Ric Flair and Superstar Billy Graham, as well as *December 8, 1980: The Day John Lennon Died*. He is a lifetime New Yorker.